Written by Lloyd Dudley Burris
All computer code, algorithms, and equations in this book are
Copyright © Lloyd Dudley Burris 2015

TABLE OF CONTENTS

TABLE OF CONTENTS

8. Verify the results and use the information

TABLE OF CONTENTS

PREFACE

This book is about a method of time travel with a computers. This is the third book in the series with time travel with computers and information. In my first two books I took my readers through a numerical system controlled by algorithms that grew out of Einstein's work with relativity that used V for information, R for the reference point viewing that information, and C for cosmological constant that controls the rate of expansion between V and R. The BNS numerical system can store a number trillions of digits or longer but the user would only have to carry the last digit of the number around. When the user was ready then the user could use BNS retrieve the rest of the number which was in theory mathematically stored in time instead of space. In essence BNS uses time has its hard drive instead of space.

In this book I will be showing the user how to use a computer to store a file as a check-sum (simple number) and use that check-sum or number to recreate the file. Then I will show the user how to take this program and feed it numbers (check-sums) to search for time travel computer media of the future, past, or other dimensions. In essence, I will teach the reader of this book how to time travel with computers. To find time travel computer media of the past, future, or other dimensions. Or to use my software to approximate analog signals of light and sound of other places in space-time so the user can view other times and places without leaving this space-time.

Also in this book I will show my readers my A/B algorithm. If A in the future and B in the past both know the weak check-sum range of their messages to each other through space-time will be in. For example C High check-sum and D low check-sum range. Then A in the future can write B in the past an email and delete it. Then B in the past can data mine the check-sum range between C and D and look for the message or messages that A in the future sent to B in the past. This is a form of temporal communication. This temporal email system can go so far as to embed temporal codes in the messages to verify the sender and receiver of those messages and could include file attachments.

My books work off the theory that there is no future, there is no past, there is only a continuum of space and time where time never ends nor does time never begin. The future and the past is a point of reference in the space-time continuum. I will explain more in the book about this. You see, the quantum uncertainty principle in physics does not prevent the past from knowing the future nor does it prevent the future from knowing the past. And quantum uncertainty does not prevent the future nor the past from knowing about other dimensions where the time-line is different. In this book when I mention other dimensions I mean other time-lines. This is how and why time travel with information and computers work. There is so much I have to teach some that wants to learn to time travel with computers and read this book. I want to dedicate this book to my beautiful wife Sheila Burris and my two wonderful children Meredith Burris and Amy Burris.

Introduction

There is another universe that very few people know about. It is a universe where all information exist. A place where all that has happened in the past exist. A place where all that is happening now exist. A place where all that will happen in the future exist. Not only in this time-line but in all time-lines in all dimensions. This universe is eternal. Never ending never beginning. A universe that exists for all time and contains information, energy, and mass. The informational universe exist because space-time has the capacity to represent this information. As long as a space-time exist in the cosmos this informational universe goes on.

If the informational universe could be explored then all creation would be at ones on finger tips. All knowledge would be for the taking. All knowledge would be for free. This is where I come in. In this book I show how to hack god's computer and take what is on the hard drive. How this is possible is by setting up a binary counter the size of a computer file. Program an algorithm to make the binary counter run. Then data mine this counter for information as it runs. Some would say this is impossible. I have spent a life time proving it's not. There are methods and tools to make this job easier and faster.

Now this type of data mining opens up a new world of possibilities that is unheard of. This creates a fifth dimensional computer simulator by which all of space-time can be explored by searching for computer media of the past, future or alternate dimensions. This fifth dimensional simulator can be used for communication with the past, future or other dimensions. Hacking computers without ever connecting to them no matter where or when they are becomes possible. Bypassing research and invention becomes possible. And this is just the tip of the iceberg. As I plan to show in this book. This ultimately could be used for bridging the gap between one part of space-time to another part of space-time making space-time itself a small world of its own. To be explored on a computer at home in the comfort of one's own home as if searching the internet.

In this book I not only talk about the cosmos but all aspects of time travel and then I will talk about time travel with computers. I need to talk about all aspects of time travel so the reader can understand the latter as well as the former. There is also a lot of computer science in this book. For the computer savvy nerd this book has everything. For the layman I will try to keep it as simple as possible. Now please come on this journey with me. A journey into time travel and time travel with computers.

How The Universe Came Into Existence.

It has been said by science that the universe came into existence. Well I do not believe that. In space and time energy is never created nor is it destroyed. It just changes from one form of energy to another. Matter itself is never created nor destroyed. Matter can become energy and energy can become matter. Matter can be transmuted to other types of matter or converted back to energy. So matter and energy are never created nor destroyed.

Even information in the universe is never created nor is it destroyed. Information changes from one from of information to another. Take my DNA in my body for example. Before I was born the information to create me existed but was not physical. I did not exist physically but I existed as information. I was born and my information that is my DNA now existed. Now, as I grow older my DNA will get changed slowly over time. I call that getting encrypted changing from my very first version of my DNA to another causing me to age and get older and we call that a normal process in life though for me that does not feel very normal but that is what the universe has giving me.

At some point in time my DNA will become so damaged that I as an individual will no longer be able to live thus I will die. But, my information was not created nor was it destroyed. My information was encrypted back into the universe. But, the information that was me will always exist whether physical or not. Some day in the future space and time will make my information physical again and thus again I will live again. Never remembering my previous lifes. And this cycle will continue forever in the continuum.

So you see there is no way our universe came into existence. Our universe is just information, energy, and matter being recycled over and over again. Now, our universe may go through different energy states and stages of development where what we know will end but at some point it will go through a stage of development and what we know will begin again.
Not only has the universe always existed but it is a perpetual motion machine the likes of which mankind can only wonder about. We may never know all its secrets in this life nor the next. We all are just passengers on a great ride that has no beginning nor no end.

The Big Bang Theory

The big bang theory states that at the beginning of space-time the universe expanded from a small little dot called a singularity and has being expanding until now around 13 billion years later. But the big bang theory has many flaws. It cannot explain what existed before the big bang. It cannot explain what will become of the universe. I think the big bang theory was a pretty good attempt to explain the universe. It certainly explained what has happened in the last 13 billion years but cannot explain what happen before that or what will happen later.

There was no explosion or bang. The name of theory is misleading. In plain language our universe at the beginning of time was a black hole that expanded into a universe. Now, we are not on the outside of this universe. No, we are inside of it as it expands. No one knows for sure right now if it will contract and expand again. The universe as we know it right now is just a kid. When it finally grows up our solar system as we know it now will not be here anymore. This is so very far into the future that we as humans if we continue will have evolved so much we will no longer look like humans at all.

At best in my view the big bang theory is a partial unfinished theory. But, it's not the whole story. It's not the whole truth about our universe. There is another truth. There is another story. It is an unsolved detective case. The case is called the missing universe case. Where was the universe 14, 15, 16 or 20 billion years ago? Where will the universe be in 20 more billion years? Nobody seems to know right now. I don't believe nothing existed before the big bang or that nothing will exist in the future. What is certain that unless we as humans escape to the stars then none of us will get off this planet alive? We can only wait and see what science learns in the future.

The Rainbow Universe

The rainbow universe is an attempt to explain the problems the big bang theory had. What the Rainbow theory says is that all particles in space-time time travel to a point in space-time according to their energy level. So, particles with higher energy's time travel to the past where the big bang happened and particles with lower energy's time travel to the future where the universe is a cold, dark, lonely, and empty place. Somewhere in between we exist. So basically all matter and energy time travels to a place in the universe according to its energy level. We are traveling at what we believe to be the future. Why particles and photons time travel is because space-time is curved by gravity. It is this curve that causes particles to time travel according to their energy levels.

The rainbow universe theory makes us all time travelers in theory. I have many questions about this theory. Does the time-line stay the same every time or does it change the next time around? This theory I can live with because it allows for a continuum that is never ending nor never beginning. Where there is no past or future there is just simply put. Time and more time and more time. Over and over again. Now, if or when this can be proven I am waiting to see eagerly. Currently a lot of scientist have problems with the rainbow gravity/universe theory. Some say it has no basis in reality. It has never been proven yet either. It is just still a theory.

Einstein-Rosen Bridge

There is another theory that states our universe is the exact opposite of a black hole known as a white hole. A white hole is a region of space-time that cannot be entered into from the outside. Light and matter can escape from it from a white hole. So this is called the reverse of a black hole. Einstein's field equations allow for the existence of white holes but science has yet to prove their existence in nature. This is one of the most believable theories of our universe existence that I know of.

The problem I have with science not being able to prove white holes is that our universe grew from a singularity and expanded outward. So, when science says it cannot prove their existence I am like hello. Is that not what happened to our universe at the supposed big bang event. The big bang for me may be our universe forming as a white hole from space-time. And, Einstein's field equations allow for this.

What more proof does science need? Some-times I scratch my head when I read science articles. The big bang is the exact same conditions as a white hole forming out of space-time that Einstein's equations allowed for. We are living inside the proof that science needs. Black holes don't last forever so if we are living in a white hole this universe won't last forever but space-time does last forever. And white holes and black holes will always find a way to form in space-time.

Our universe comes from a 4-dimensional universe

This theory states that our universe is the birth of after a 4-dimensional star collapsed into a black hole and ejected debris. Our 3D space-time is those debris. So our universe is floating as a membrane in a 4 dimensional universe. So our universe is the 3D event horizon of a 4D black hole. The expansion of our universe is the event horizon of the 4D black whole as it feeds. This theory still has its own problems which scientist are trying to figure out. For me I think this theory is on the right track. I often wonder if a lot of these theories are one in the same as the other theories that I read.

I wonder could a white hole as Einstein believed it is the same theory this theory is trying to understand. Could not white holes be the dimensional event horizon of a black hole in an upper dimensional universe? Could this be how white holes are formed that science has yet to explain? That is my theory. Some of these theories could use other theories to help mathematically prove them I think.

Time and space tied to universe creation

Whatever the theory of our universe there is one law of physics that cannot be broken. Now, this is my law of physics. Whatever happens in physics cannot just happen one time. Again, whatever happens in physics cannot just happen one time. It is not physically possible. Whatever really created our universe is a process that is repeatable. So, we know three things.

1   A process created our universe.
2   It is not physically possible for anything in physics to happen just one time.
3   Thus we all live in a continuum where there is no beginning nor end to space-time.

Somewhere somehow space-time is tied to the creation, destruction, and rebirth of all things in our universe and beyond. Yes our universe is violent but out of violence comes life and death but it is a never ending cycle of life and death for all things. We all play our part in that. At one time our atomic particles were in a sun. Maybe at one time our particles existed as an asteroid or comet. Then we existed as dirt in the earth then we came to live as a human being. Then we will return to the earth and eventually return to the universe to repeat that cycle all over again. Someday on another earth somewhere in space-time this cycle will eventually repeat again.

With time never ending nor beginning and the fact that nothing can happen just one time it is a

100 percent possibility that we well all live again someday over and over.

So we will all get the chance to live out every possible combination of possible lives for eternity though for us it always seem like the first time. I have seen young people party enjoying their youths and their life's saying to themselves "We will never be here again". Well no not that they remember but in the history of space-time they have always been here. Partying and saying that over and over "We will never be here again". Whether or not we will be here again is a matter of perspective. We are all just travelers moving from one plane of existence to another plane of existence throughout eternity. We will always be here again and again.

What is time travel?

Time travel is the movement of information, energy, or matter. Any one of these or all of these from an area in space and time to another area in space and time. Time travel unknown to the average person does not require that a person physically travel in time. All time travel requires is the movement of something from one area in space-time to another area in space-time.

That is time travel. Something traveling or moving through time. In a sense we are all time travelers. We move at what we perceive to be forward in time. Now that does not mean that time travel to the past is impossible. Time itself is a point of reference. Anything that is before that reference is in the past and anything after that reference is in the future. So, to travel in time we need three things. A reference point, the movement of time, and something to move through time. Then we have time travel. As for causality violations that is a side effect of time travel. Just like the sonic boom is a side effect of traveling faster than the speed of sound.

Understanding time travel

There are many misunderstandings about time travel. The first misunderstanding is that time travel has to be physical but that is not true. It is possible to stay in our own time-line and look at the past, future, or alternate realities as I will further show ahead in this book.

The next misunderstanding is that we have to travel to the past to travel backwards in time. No, not true. You see space-time is a continuum. It is very possible to travel into the future to a point where the earth exist and is going through the same time-line as it is going through now. So, it would be possible to travel into the future to a future earth to get back oh let's say to 1945 World War II. And as science knows now it is very possible to time travel to the future. Unlike traveling to the past which is even harder it is much easier to travel to the future. So, we can get back to the past by going forward in time.

The easiest way by far to time travel is with computers as I will show in this book. We can use computers to see the future, past, alternate time lines and even other parts of space-time. All that without even leaving the house. I do it all the time every day. With time travel with computers these things are possible:

    A. The movement of information through space-time or the decryption of a computer file that was created in the past or will be created in the future.

    B. Using a binary counters to approximate analog signals of another place in space-time as a computer media file all that is very possible.

The movement of information from one area in space-time to this area in space-time by way of computers is a form of time travel. You see, I use binary counters to approximate analog signals or computer files from other times and places as a form of time travel with computers. Thus, I turned my computer into a time machine.

Time is a continuum. The future is just a point of reference in this continuum and the past is the same. In reality the future nor the past does not exist as we know it because time is forever and so is space, energy, matter, and information. It all last forever changing over and over.

Now, I do not discount physical time travel to the past. I am sure somewhere in the laws of physics that is possible with enough energy. But, just like I said it is possible to travel to the future to get to the past the same is true for time travel to the past. We can travel to the past to an earth that is going through the same time-line as our own to a point in our future that our current earth has not gotten to yet.

So, when traveling to the past it is possible to travel to the future from time travel to the past. It is just a matter of perspective because the time-line stretches to eternity in both directions where both the future and the past exist in either direction. So, in a sense it really does not matter which way you travel in time either way you can reach both the future or the past. And, our universe has provided a way to time-travel. If we reach the speed of light time stops. So, at the speed of light we can go anywhere in the universe and in theory anywhere in the time-line that we want. Just by going forward in time and reaching the speed of light.

And as with time travel don't discount going to that alternate time-line. Now, what about a time traveler going to the past and killing his or her parents would that kill them? Well I so far do not believe that. All time travel does is transfer something through space-time to another space-time.

Once there all the laws of physics still apply. No, I don't believe if someone traveled to the past and killed their parents they would disappear. Because all time travel does is transfer information, matter, or energy anyone of these things are all of these things through time.

Now the time-line will change. But the time traveler would be fine as long as no one kills them too. There won't be another of them born at least just yet. But, the time traveler by the very act of killing his or her parents erased their future and created another one. But they will be fine. They will not disappear.

Time travel is just the simple transfer of information, energy, or matter. Nothing more nothing less. The grand farther paradox is solved but viewing time travel as just a simple transfer and a change in the events in the time-line.

A time-line is a string of reference points viewing their information. If the point of reference is changed this changes the real time-line after that point of reference is changed. Read my BNS if you have not done so already. Just the very act of time travel changes the time-line.

Time-lines and time travel is just the points of reference viewing its information. In my time-line when I was with my parents they were still alive. I was viewing my information as a point of reference. Then for the sake of argument I traveled to the past and killed my parents. Now they are dead in the past. I am the reference point and my parents are the information. I still exist as information viewed by reference points which is other people and objects are around me even if I just killed my parents before I was born. My future is now erased and a new future exist. I still live but I will not be born again. My parents would be gone and the future would be changed. And most likely that future would be me spending the rest of my life in prison and people wondering who the heck I really am and where I really come from.

Time and space and time travel and time lines is information that changes over time for ever and ever. If I time travel I am a reference point viewing my information and I can change that information and thus change the time-line. If I time-travel and change something that is no different than changing something in the time-line before I time traveled. There is no difference and no grandfather paradox to solve. The only thing that is different is the information contained in the time-line. It can be erased and re-written like a record-able CD or DVD. The time-line does not care. The time-line is just a string of reference points observing their information. That is all. Nothing more.

Physics of time travel

Albert Einstein

Albert Einstein was a theoretical physicist that lived from March 14, 1879 to April 18, 1955. He was German born and he developed the general theory of relativity. Einstein's theory is also known as SR or STR that is short for special theory of relativity. SR sets out the fundamental relationship between space and time. SR states that gravity is a property of space-time and is related to whatever energy and mass are present. More importantly for this book Einstein showed how the passage of time can be affected by gravity. He showed that the faster a person goes the slower time passes for that person. Einstein theorized the existence of black holes and predicts gravitational waves. SR is the most modern theory of space-time that we have alongside quantum mechanics.

Theory of Relativity

In Einstein's theory of relativity space can effect energy and matter and energy and matter can effect space. There is a speed limit to light. Einstein had a cosmological constant in his equations to explain the contraction or expansion of space. The most important thing as far as the book is concerned is that gravity and mass can change the rate at which time flows. So, can speed and or acceleration.

In Einstein's theory the thing that impressed me the most was his train thought experiment. Where a point of reference observes its information and that the point of reference can move with its information in time. And the cosmological constant which can be used to mathematically control the rate of expansion or contraction of space-time in Einstein's equations. I used Einstein's cosmological constant in my BNS to control the rate of expansion or contraction between V and R in my BNS equations.

Summing Up My Theory of the Universe

1   We live in a continuum.
2   There is no past except with a point of reference.
3   There is no future except with a point of reference.
4   There exist in time in the fourth dimension an informational universe.
5   The informational universe is where the past and the future reside and everything else.
6   The informational universe is accessible by way of my BNS and my time travel computer programs. Which I plan to put up for public licensing on my web-site http://time-travel.institute in the near future.
7   Information along with energy and matter is never created nor destroyed. It just changes.

I have more theories but they are outside the scope of this book. But, to make things interesting I will go ahead and put some of them here because they do deal with time travel.
Let's start with what I think gravity really is. Gravity is the interaction between matter and the energy spectrum of the universe. That would be the entire EMF energy spectrum from radio waves, to light, to radiation.

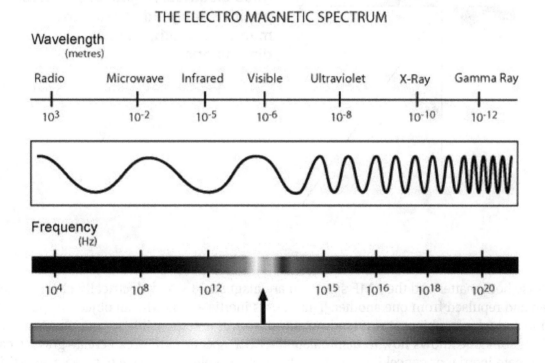

SR says gravity is the result of energy and mass so I believe that SR backs me up when I get very specific as I do about gravity. A serious scientist has to take into account the entire EMF energy spectrum to account for gravity. Now, how is the possible someone might ask?

You see matter is made up of positive, negative and neutral charges. Even when you break down neutral charges their particles too can contain charges. And matter is also made up of magnetically south and magnetically north particles.

The EMF spectrum as it propagates through the universe it goes electrically positive, electrically negative, magnetically positive, and magnetically negative.

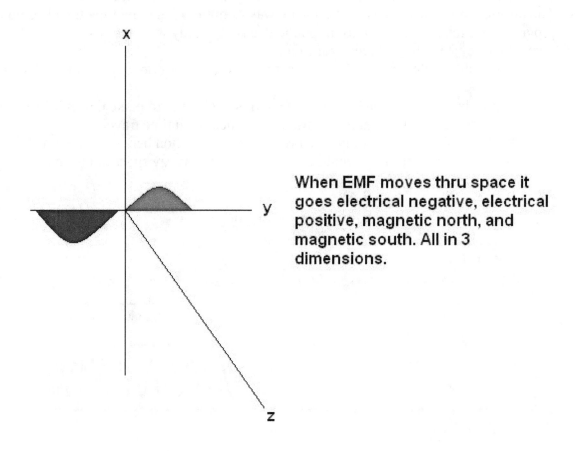

When EMF moves thru space it goes electrical negative, electrical positive, magnetic north, and magnetic south. All in 3 dimensions.

So because both matter and the EMF spectrum are magnetically and electrically charged they are attracted and repulsed from one another. This causes inertia and is why an object in space stays in motion and why an object at rest tends to stay at rest. It is responsible for our physics as we know it. If someone knows how to manipulate the EMF spectrum they can create gravity, cancel gravity, create inertia, or cancel inertia. It is why if one accelerates in space it create an artificial gravity like on a spinning space-station. That is the interaction of matter with the EMF spectrum of space which we know as gravity. The EMF spectrum tends to hold a body at rest so as a body spends in a circle or accelerates that body feels itself held back or held down by the EMF spectrum. This is the electrical/magnetic charges in the body interacting with the electrical/magnetic charges of the EMF spectrum. A body in motion can't slow down unless something makes it slow down. And a body at rest can't speed up unless something makes it speed up. The EMF spectrum is like the glue of space-time. It holds onto mass and interacts with mass. Mass in turn follows the EMF spectrum of space like magnet going through a gauss-gun.

The aether of space - Time

```
N S - + N S - + N S - + N S - + N S - + N S - +
N S - + N S - + N S - + N S - + N S - + N S - +
N S - + N S - + N S - + N S - + N S - + N S - +
N S - + N S - + N S - + N S - + N S - + N S - +
N S - + N S - + N S - + N S - + N S - + N S - +
N S - + N S - + N S - + N S - + N S - + N S - +
N S - + N S - + N S - + N S - + N S - + N S - +
N S - + N S - + N S - + N S - + N S - + N S - +
N S - + N S - + N S - + N S - + N S - + N S - +
N S - + N S - + N S - + N S - + N S - + N S - +
N S - + N S - + N S - + N S - + N S - + N S - +
N S - + N S - + N S - + N S - + N S - + N S - +
N S - + N S - + N S - + N S - + N S - + N S - +
N S - + N S - + N S - + N S - + N S - + N S - +
N S - + N S - + N S - + N S - + N S - + N S - +
N S - + N S - + N S - + N S - + N S - + N S - +
N S - + N S - + N S - + N S - + N S - + N S - +
N S - + N S - + N S - + N S - + N S - + N S - +
N S - + N S - + N S - + N S - + N S - + N S - +
```

The EMF propagation thru space causes electrical-magnetic vector path ways for matter to follow because matter has both electrical and magnetic properties.

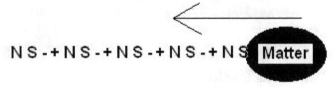

N S - + N S - + N S - + N S - + N S [Matter]

So, the more mass there is the more charges and magnetic polls there is at the sub-atomic level. Well the EMF spectrum of the universe bends to mass BECAUSE BOTH MASS AND THE EMF SPECTRUM HAVE ELECTRICAL CHARGES AND MAGNETIC POLLS.
So, matter follows the EMF spectrum of the universe. The EMF spectrum bends into planets and stars that is the lines of space. Matter follows the EMF spectrum because the EMF spectrum is the fabric of space-time itself. Without energy or mass there is no gravity. So the EMF spectrum is what bends to mass to create what we know as gravity. Mass follows the EMF spectrum as lines of space-time or as the fabric of space-time.

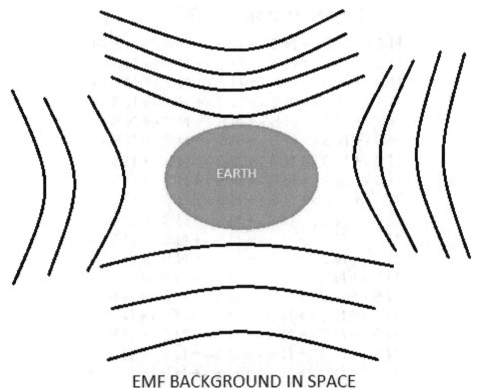

EMF BACKGROUND IN SPACE
CREATES GRAVITY!!!!!!!!!!!!!!!

Matter has electrons which have north and south magnetic poles. Matter also has protons which are electrical positive and electrons which are electrical negative. EMF propagates in 3D space as Magnet North and South and Electrical positive and negative. This EMF propagates at different frequencies. Thes frequences allow matter to follow the electrical magnetic lines EMF in space. Now, when matter clumps together its charges start adding up in a way as to distort the EMF background of space.

So, objects fall to larger objects because THAT IS WHERE THE EMF LINES OF SPACE TAKE THEM.

So, you won't read the specific as I represented them anywhere else unless someone has stolen my work. So GRAVITY = THE ELECTRICAL AND MAGNETIC INTERACTION BETWEEN THE EMF SPECTRUM OF THE UNIVERSE AND MATTER. That is what gravity is. Gravity waves = The EMF spectrum of the universe moving together like the waves on an Ocean. That is what the EMF spectrum is. An OCEAN OF ENERGY!!!

Now I believe the reason the universe is still expanding is because the big bang is still happening. It never stopped. Energy is coming into the universe. Black holes are sucking energy out of the universe. When the big bang finally stops black holes and gravity will take over and the universe will start contracting again into a singularity. Once the contraction is finished which will take a very long time then the universe will begin its life again in another big bang.

Expansion and Contraction of our Universe

Universe

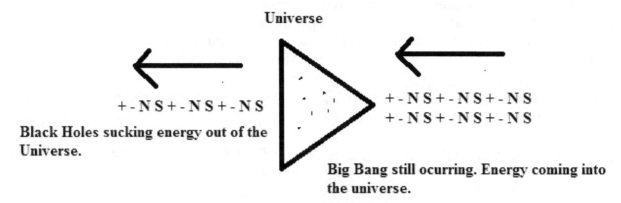

+ - N S + - N S + - N S

Black Holes sucking energy out of the Universe.

+ - N S + - N S + - N S
+ - N S + - N S + - N S

Big Bang still ocurring. Energy coming into the universe.

The Big Bang is still ocurring. There is more energy coming into the Universe than leaving so the Universe is expanding. Black holes are sucking the energy out of the Universe. When energy stops coming into the Universe black holes will and gravity will take over and the Universe will contract into a singularity again. The big bang will begin again.

The EMF spectrum of the universe is free energy for the taken but in today's society free energy is largely illegal because you can't put a meter on it and charge people money. Those who have tried to bring free energy to the public have been silenced and will continue to be silenced.

So, YES THE EMF SPECTRUM CAN BE HARNESSED AS A SOURCE OF ENERGY. It is very complicated but it can be done but done so at one's own peril in today's society. Oil companies have no intention of going out of business. The banking industry which regulates the USA economy has its hands in big oil. So, the oil industry is part of the banking system and part of the government it can't be put out of business.

Big oil is the banking system and big oil is the government. So, don't look for free energy anytime soon even though Tesla proved it existed and attempted at his peril and ruin to bring it to mankind. So too have a long line of inventors after him have tried and failed to bring free energy to the public. Not because they couldn't but because of the silent law that free energy is illegal. If you can't put a meter on it and charge people money to use it then it is forbidden and illegal.

We live in a world where someone will always control the food, water, and energy and tell others that they have to pay them for it if they want it. It is not that food, water, and energy can't be free it is just that humans are too greedy and power hungry to have a better society where we are all equal and the same.

Oh we have tried to create societies like that. Communism and capitalism are those creations and both have never proved to be a perfect way for mankind to live. I have read about a resource based economy where the supply always equal the demand. Where there is no currency and everyone works and is equal. Housing, doctors, food, water, and energy are all free in this type of society. Pollution and the other problems of society be like homeless people and poverty would no longer exist. But, the greed and power side of humanity will never allow us to have a resource based society where we all work and everything is free and the old, sick, and elderly are taken care of. No one in this society though would get a pay check but no one would want for anything either. So, this ends the discussion of free energy. Moving on……

The EMF spectrum can be manipulated by high energy. On YouTube search for the Hutchinson effect. I have two theories on the Hutchinson effect.

1. He either setup a curved EMF field with his instruments that functioned as an artificial curved space-time which caused his objects to float.

2. He caused the matter to vibrate which created gravity waves. Gravity waves can carry away the momentum of an object as energy. Gravity waves can give an object positive or negative momentum with respect to a second source of gravity which is the earth.

3. Or, his experiments were a combination of 1 and 2. I tend to believe this is the case.

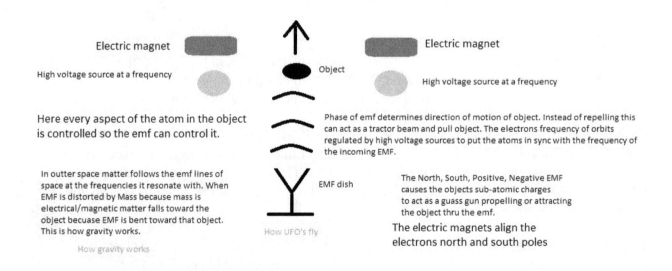

Electric magnet

High voltage source at a frequency

Here every aspect of the atom in the object is controlled so the emf can control it.

In outer space matter follows the emf lines of space at the frequencies it resonate with. When EMF is distorted by Mass because mass is electrical/magnetic matter falls toward the object becuase EMF is bent toward that object. This is how gravity works.

How gravity works

Object

Phase of emf determines direction of motion of object. Instead of repelling this can act as a tractor beam and pull object. The electrons frequency of orbits regulated by high voltage sources to put the atoms in sync with the frequency of the incoming EMF.

EMF dish

How UFO's fly

Electric magnet

High voltage source at a frequency

The North, South, Positive, Negative EMF causes the objects sub-atomic charges to act as a guass gun propelling or attracting the object thru the emf.

The electric magnets align the electrons north and south poles

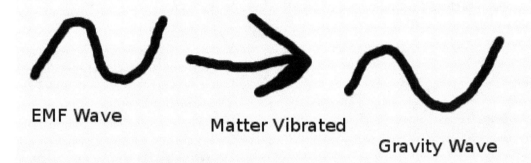

EMF Wave   Matter Vibrated
                              Gravity Wave

EMF wave converted to gravity wave

SR or STR shows that matter and space are interconnected. EMF can vibrate matter which in turn creates gravity waves. Matter also follows the lines of space which is the entire EMF background. This more specifically is why we have gravity. UFO's which yes they are real and exist and yes we are being visited by Aliens. I am sorry to tell the public and this is no joke or laughing matter. It is real. The Aliens space-ships or UFO's as we call them can make their ships act like a Gauss-Gun to propel it through the EMF spectrum of space . O > North, South, Negative, Positive all their space-ship has to do is manipulate its electrical/magnetic fields to achieve propulsion or warp drive. And, according to conspiracy theorist this is currently what the USA military is working on for space-craft and the next generation fighter air craft. Either gravity waves or the Bio-Field Brown effect and in fact the Hutchinson effect can be used for space-craft propulsion. On YouTube there is a video about an Alien Reproduction Space-craft. If you have not seen it I highly advise you to watch it. It uses capacitors shaped like a pie slice in a circle about 5 layers deep. They charge up to a million volts and use the Bio-Field brown effect for propulsion but at the same time the high energy warps space making faster than light speed possible.

Now, here is a picture I found of a UFO on the internet years and years ago.

Hutchinson in his experiments also caused wood and metal to melt together. KINDA LIKE WHAT HAPPENED IN THE PHILLIDELPHA EXPERIMENT!!! HUH, WHO WOULD OF THOUGHT? The Hutchison effect verified for me that parts of the story of the PHILLIDELPA experiment were true because the Hutchison effect was a real life verified experiment that had some of the same results as what happened in the Philadelphia experiment.

So, to physically time travel one needs to know that the EMF spectrum can be broken up into dimensions where part of those dimensions act as space and part of those dimensions act as time. If one can create a complex energy field that acts with the EMF spectrum of space-time then one can time-travel, travel into other dimensions, create star gates. Zip across the universe faster than the speed of light. All that stuff.

The Bio-Field brown effect of charging capacitors up to Hugh amounts of energy can be used for propulsion and warping of space-time. The Hutchinson effect employed large tesla coils and radar to create his effects he did not use large capacitors that I know of which was probably good for him. I think Hutchinson was one step from finding himself back in the age of the dinosaurs. Had he used more high energy equipment no telling what would of happen. He could have made his entire apartment complex disappear and move across the country.

The man who performed the Hutchinson effect did get the cops called on him because he was making stuff float in his neighbor's apartment. Now, I do find that incredibly funny. Just think how mad his neighbors would have been if his apartment complex was transported across the country. I am sure they would have felt some kind of way about that. What if they would have being transported and went back in time too. I am sure he would have been running for his life after everyone figured out he did it.

So, this is some of the things that can happen if someone plays with high energy. The USA learned that the hard way In the Philadelphia experiment and so too was it learned with the Hutchinson effect and so too was it learned with the Bio-Field brown effect. When people play with high energy they play with the EMF spectrum of the universe thus they play with space, time, and gravity itself. They go into Einstein's territory with no knowledge of physics and how to get themselves out of a bad situation if they screw up. So, besides being deadly high energy causes space-time anomalies. Which I am pretty sure is being experimented in secret by governments right now. High energy does cause space-time anomalies and yes space-time can be experimented with using high energy. That would be electrical, magnetic, and with EMF. All these things can warp space-time.

Experimenting with space-time via high energy can be used for good or for evil. Imagine a secret branch of the government that can go back in time and erase people from the time-line. What about a real temporal war between governments. These are some things the Geneva Convention does not cover. Nor do any treaties between governments. China is the first country in the world that has actually publically out-lawed time travel. And for good reason. If one or more of their citizens could time travel they could keep the communist government from coming to power.

But experimenting with space-time via high energy can be used for good to. It could be used to develop deep space travel. It can be used to look into the future and foresee earthquakes and volcano eruptions before they happen and get people out of harm's way. It can be used to develop free energy. It can be used for good too.

But to be honest. It is my belief this is what is at the heart of all the classified budgets and projects that not even the president of the United States nor members of congress gets to see or hear about.

Now to finish off why I believe we live in a continuum. Besides the law of physics which I came up with that says nothing in physics can only happen once. We live in a continuum because energy, matter, and information can never be created nor destroyed. It just keeps changing from one form to another. That pretty much sounds like a continuum to me does it not? That pretty much says to me that nothing in physics can only happen once.

Yep, so somewhere in the future throughout eternity I will be back here writing this book again. I have probably written this book no telling how many times but it is not possible for me to remember because I am matter and information and I am destined to be recycled as is the way of life. My memories are only of this life not the next or the previous life.

But, when I get recycled I will not experience time between my death and next birth. For me it will be instantaneous. Now some people believe in ghost and spirits. I have a theory about that too. There is dark matter and dark energy besides our normal matter and energy universe. Who is to say that when our normal matter body is recycled that another copy does not exist as dark matter or as a shadow upon the normal fabric of space-time. The universe is incredibly complex. So who knows? I know there is an explanation that science can explain but that kind of science is still a long way off. In the end I believe like the universe we all experience different planes of existence. The universe goes through different states of energy in its existence which is a never ending cycle. But we as living beings go through different planes of existence in a never ending cycle. This is the way life is in the continuum.

Time is real

The one aspect about time is no one can get away from it. No matter where one runs they cannot escape time. Even if they travel in time as we know it time will still always be there for them. To really understand the permanence of time we can look at ancient Egypt and Rome and the ancient Samaria civilization. These civilizations lasted for a very long time. They even in their minds thought their civilizations would be around forever. But, with the passage of time it was proven that time catches up with everything. Everything has its own time where it exist then has its own time where it is gone.

That was true for the dinosaurs, which was true for ancient Egypt, ancient Rome, and ancient Samaria. It will be true for mankind and the earth. Time is so permanent and so real that time is in its own right is a force of its own. The unseen force no one nor nothing can run from. No government, no civilization, no one species on earth can run from time. Time is the great creator and the great destroyer of all things. Time is the continuum's police force. Time has no special feelings. Time targets everything randomly. The only thing that can stop time is gravity and mass but even then time still catches up to gravity and mass too. All black holes though they can exist for a very long time even they will someday fade away. Time will catch up with them too. Time will catch up with all planets and the universe itself.

If anything in this universe if more permanent and more real and more unstoppable that is father time. Time is the grim reaper that comes for all things sooner or later. Nothing can escape father time. Nothing. Time itself is the greatest force that can ever exist even greater than our own universe and gravity and energy and matter. Time is the greatest force of them all.

At the beginning of our current cycle of the universe when the universe expanded the fourth dimension we know as time was sent out in all directions as a wave. That is what the arrow of time its. The arrow of time is a wave which we ride in one direction to what we know of as the future. Like a surfer at a beach catching a wave.

The reason time slows as one approaches the speed of light is the same theory as riding a boat on a lake. As the boat moves it is hitting waves on the top of the lake. In our universe we are hitting time waves as we move forward. Every time we touch one of these waves time advances forward. But, now on the lake as the boat goes faster and faster it starts skipping and skimming across the top of the lake. Skipping waves. That is the same in our universe. The faster we move we skip over the waves of time. Every-time we skip a wave time does not advance forward.

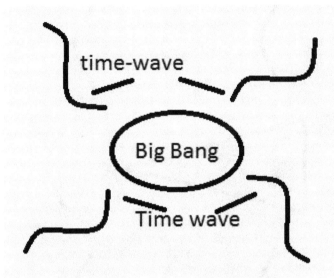

time-wave

Big Bang

Time wave

Time wave, Warp time wave, better known as THE ARROW OF TIME.

Science has been trying to understand the arrow of time. Like warp-drive we can have a time-drive. At the beginning of the big bang a time-wave was created. All of space-time is caught up in this wave which is why time only goes forward. To time travel backwards this wave would have to be cancled and a artifical time wave established. going backwards in time.

Why time slows down as we go faster and faster.

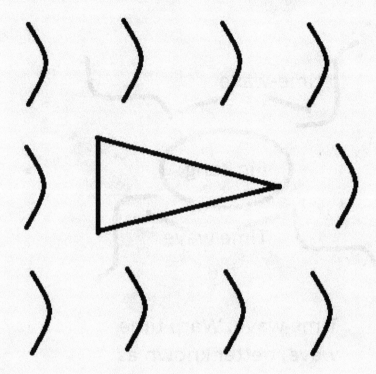

Space time is like a lake or a ocean. As we go faster we skip across the waves. Ever wave we skip momentarly stops time for us in little slices so time slows down. At the speed of light we are no longer hitting any waves so time stops completely.

METHODS OF TIME TRAVEL

Infinite Cylinder

It has been thought in science to be a possible means of time travel. It was thought of as a solution to Einstein's SR. It allows for time-travel in a rotating cylinder because of closed time-like curves caused by frame dragging. As the cylinder rotates it drags space-time around with it in a circle until a certain point is reached where time-travel is possible. As is with the field of science other scientist have come forward to point out certain flaws this method of time travel may have. But, it is one of the ways to time travel that has been mathematically proven. Strangely enough other methods of time travel also employ frame dragging as their method of time travel. Then they try to claim this is something new. No its not. It is just another version of the Infinite Cylinder theory talked about in a different way.

Black Holes

Black holes are the most ready to use time machines in the universe. Their best use is for traveling to the future. All someone has to do is park their space-ship outside of the event horizon and orbit the black hole and come out of orbit in the future. It is possible to travel thousands of years into the future this way.

Since black holes warp time into a circle it may be possible to orbit the hole at such a speed as to travel backwards in time. This is called an infinite cylinder. The black hole pulls space-time around it as it spins. So a time traveler would have to counter rotate with the black hole at a fast enough velocity. Now time for the time traveler would slow down inside the ship but outside the ship time would be going backwards as the ship pierces the 3 dimensions of space and physically enters the 4th dimension of time in the reverse direction.

Cosmic Strings

Cosmic strings are thought to be cracks in the fabric of space-time of our underlying universe. They have been thought of as 1 dimensional and as highly dimensional. The theory surrounding cosmic strings is very vast to say the least and this book cannot do the subject of cosmic strings justice as to the scope of the subject. But, cosmic strings have been thought of as a way to travel in time and space.

Quantum Entanglement

This method would use entangling two particles through time so that if a person in the future moves the particle the person in the past will observe that movement. And, if the person in the past moves that particle the person in the future would observe that movement. That is rather over simplified but it explains my point the best. This method could be used for temporal communication. Now there is more to this but that will get explained later on in this book.

Warping Space-Time

Warping space takes at least a million volts of electricity. Contrary to what the public knows yes it is very possible to use high energy and build a machine to warp space but the public is not supposed to know about it and for good reason. SOMEONE MIGHT TRY IT! It is scientifically possible to warp space on the ground to slow time down or speed time up. The effect would be like being in a space-ship going very fast in space except the pilot would be on the ground sitting in a machine bolted to the ground. A machine that looks like a gyro scope except all the moving pieces conduct high amounts of energy with the pilot sitting in the middle would fit the bill for how something like that might look and work.

With two or more of these machines running at the same time it might be possible to create an artificial warm hole or star gate where the time traveler could walk through the middle of the machines to travel in space-time.

Currently science is looking at warping space for space-travel but warping space has many uses of such as time travel, artificial worm holes, and star gates. All these machines could be constructed from devices that can warp space-time.

Time Machines

A true time machine is one that can be on a planet sitting still and be useful by an individual or individuals that want to travel in time. It would have to warp the first 3 dimensions of space-time into a bubble and catch a ride on the river of time in the 4th dimension. It would need a means of propulsion in the fourth dimension and also a means of propulsion in the first 3 dimensions of space. That propulsion would have to be electro-magnetic and or gravitational.

 A true time machine would and could be much more than what normal people perceive one to be. It could act as a star-gate between worlds and act as a time machine too. It could move between two points in space-time fast enough to be an artificial worm hole.

Also, space-time is a continuum there is really no such thing as a future or a past that is just a notion people invented. The future or the past is represented by a point of reference. So with that said it is possible to use a time machine to travel to the past to get to the future and use a time machine to travel to the future to get to the past because the universe is really a continuum. Time travel can get very weird. And yes it is possible to time travel to the past to get to the past and time travel to the future to get to the future. That would be the shortest distance between two points but not necessarily the only way to do it. Remember, a time-line is just a set of events happening in a specific order. Since the universe is a continuum time-lines get repeated all the time.

Worm Holes

Worm holes have been mathematically proven to be a very valid means not only of time travel but for space travel as well. The theory involved in using one would be to open up a micro-worm hole that already exist.

My theory for using them involves creating an artificial worm hole by way of warping space. It has also been side that black holes might could be used as a worm hole but they are very violent by nature and anyone trying that probably is looking at a one way trip that could be a suicide mission.

Black holes crush matter to infinity. It could be a very unpleasant way to go. Stuck like a fly in a spider web except going down the ultimate trash compacter. And with all the time in the world to think about what is going to happen. Yeah, I would pass on this.

Space Ships

Space-ships would be the best time machines of them all. If they have warp drive they can travel in space and time anywhere they want to go. They can also use black holes and stars and gas giants to pull off maneuver's that could throw them forward or backwards in time. They can also just simply go fast enough to slow time down and travel hundreds or thousands of years into the future. A space-ship could ride curved space-time like a surfer at a beach riding the waves. There would be nowhere in space-time a good space-ship could not go.

Computers

This is my preferred method of time travel. My method uses computers to search the informational universe for computer files of the past, present, future, and alternate time-lines. Other examples of computers time traveling would simulate a virtual world where a time line takes place and the events in that time line are observable in scientific detail. What my method of time travel does is use a computer to roll a binary counter. (A counter is a list of numbers from 0 to 255. That is what all computer files are.) Then data mine that counter for time travel computer media files of the present, past, future, or alternate time-lines. This method is referred to as a time travel simulator, 5th dimension simulator, temporal hacking, hacking god's computer, and the list goes on and on.

CURRENT TIME TRAVEL RESEARCH

Ronald Mallett

He is an American theoretical physicist best known for his method of time travel in the mass media. His method of time travel involved using circulating light or lasers to create a space-time loop. At one point I thought he was actually building this but I have not heard much about it since then.

Other Time Travel Research projects

I wanted to put other real life time-travel research projects here but I was not able to find any publicly. Ron Mallet was the closest I got to current time travel research besides my own. So, I will talk about my current time travel research project. Basically what I have done is used a weak and strong check-sum to reconstruct computer files. With weak and strong check-sums I have a way to perform math to calculate the weak and strong check-sums of computer files that exist in other parts of space-time. Once I calculate the weak and strong check-sum of a time travel media file it is just a matter of constructing that file with the same weak and strong check-sum. Once the file is reconstructed and the file is verified as a time travel media file then time travel has been accomplished. Moving information from one part of space-time to another. To boldly go on my computer where no man or woman has gone before.

Theories of Time Travel

Many Worlds Theories

The many world's theories states that if someone did travel in time they would create a whole new dimension for that time travel. The time traveler in the new dimension would not be effected and anything the time traveler did would be a whole new time line all together. The time traveler would be safe and the time-line the time traveler left would be safe. The new time-line created would be a whole new pathway in space and time. The old time-line would still exist in another dimension.

Grand Farther Paradox

Science has often wondered what would happen if a person went back in time and killed their grandfather. Would they disappear? Would they still be born? What would happen to the time-line? Many questions go unanswered. This is the most famous paradox of time travel and the most highly quoted when time travel is talked about.

Is Time Travel Possible?

Yes time travel is possible. It has been proven that the gravity of a black hole can stop or slow time. It has been proven mathematically that it is possible to physically travel backwards in time. It has been proven by Einstein that if you travel at the speed of light time will stop for you but you can travel decades, hundreds of years, or even thousands of years into the future. In fact at the speed of light there is nowhere in the universe someone could not go. The only problem is the universe would not keep the same clock as the person going at the speed of light.

There is more than one way to travel in time. The easiest way is to leave the planet and travel at or close to the speed of light. In star trek they took their ship around the sun and pulled away very fast to travel backwards in time. Does this really work? I do not know for sure and no one has tried it but that method had its own theory.

It is said the USA has experimented with time travel. On the Internet you can find information about project looking glass, the Philadelphia experiment, and pictures of people in the past that are out of place for the time. Then there is my own time travel with computers and information that this book is about.

Safe to say that time travel is very possible with a variety of methods. I am pretty sure that there are plenty of experiments going on around the world trying to build time machines and there may have already been some built. If my computer qualifies as a time machine then yes a time machine has been built. You can build a time machine too with your commuter I will show you later in this book how to do that.

Time Travel to the Past Not Proven Yet

Even though we do know time travel is possible to the future it has not been physically proven yet that time travel to the past is possible yet. Now, I can prove with time travel with information that it is possible to transfer information from the future to the present but to transfer energy and or matter to the past has not been proven in the pubic world yet. Now, that does not mean the secret black government of the USA has not done it there are certainly rumors about that but nothing physically proven.

It takes a great deal of energy to time travel physically. Anyone person or government who can do that you are not going to find in a phone book. Chances are if time travel to the past is being done it is classified and or being performed in secret and no one will never hear about it.

Informational Time Travel Is Proven

Here I will talk about informational time travel. Before I can talk about time travel with information let me talk about the penny experiment. The penny experiment is what proves time travel with information is possible. The penny experiment is what proves that the uncertainty principle in physics does not prevent the past or the future from being known. Here is how the penny experiments works.

OK, tomorrow at 1pm someone named john is going to flip a penny. John wants to know what results he will get. So today John takes his penny and he flips it and keeps flipping it until he gets every possible combination of his results. John found that when he flips the penny he gets heads or tails. Now, John knows the future before it has happened. John knows tomorrow when he flips that penny it will be heads or tails. John does not know which one specifically he will get but he does know the possible outcome results. Welcome to time travel with information.

So now it is tomorrow at 1pm. John flips that penny. Surprise he got heads. But John knew yesterday that he would get heads or tails just not which one. John knew the future before it happened as close as possible as it was possible to know the future. This is a informational form of time travel. This is what I do with computers except the information I deal with can be text, videos, or audio, or special files. My files can be news programs that will get broad-casted next week or next year or years from now. It's the penny experiment on steroids sort of speaking.

So, with a penny we showed how information can be transferred from the future to the past. I will be going into greater detail in this book. More so than some readers might prefer. I have with the penny experiment proven that time travel with information is possible.

The penny experiment can be done in reverse to. Let's say Joe flipped a penny yesterday. John wants to know what Joe got. Well John can take a penny and flip it until he gets all possible combinations of results. Now, John may not know what specific result Joe got but John will have the possible results Joe got. So, John transferred information from the past to the future.

Now, John has used the penny to time travel to the future and to time travel to the past. Hey, don't laugh just yet. My computer programs make it possible to construct possible emails people may have received or written. Some of that stuff gets very personal. There are those out there that do not think my technology is very funny.

Like the penny experiment I may not know what specific emails a specific person may get or write but my programs can construct the results and somewhere in the data base will be that very personal email someone may not want shared with the world. So, yes time travel with information can be light and humorous or it can be very serious and not very funny at all.

Now, before we move on I should go ahead and explain to my readers why time travel with information can construct computer files of the present, past, future, or other dimensions. First of all quantum uncertainty does not prevent the present from knowing the past or the future. Remember the penny experiment I just talked about? Quantum uncertainty played no part in finding his possible results the next day and quantum uncertainty played no part in John finding out what Joe's possible results were. Quantum uncertainty does not care if someone knows the future or the past.

Now a computer file is just a list of numbers from 0 to 255. So, let's say Joe shoots a digital film of his mother's birthday. He puts it on his home computer. He wants to look at it with his hex editor. So Joe runs his he editor and discovers wow, his mother's birthday party video is just a bunch of numbers from 0 to 255. It takes three of those numbers to define a colored dot on a computer screen which is displayed as a series of images that quickly change to make a video. All the numbers do is tell what color each dot should be. The numbers also represent audio sounds as well. Basically the numbers are just a digital representation of light and audio. And that is the video of Joe's mother's birthday party.

So, what my programs do like the penny experiment is construct files with numbers from 0 to 255 and my data mining robots look at that file to see if it has a file format and to see if it is a computer media file of the future, past, or other something else in space-time has been found. I have made a science of constructing computer files that may be from the future or the past. This is how my programs works. Like time traveling with the penny experiment now it is possible to time travel with computers instead of pennies. And the information is much more interesting and complex than just heads or tails.

Time travel with information can construct files that exist on other computers without ever connecting to that computer. No matter how sensitive or classified or protected no computer file in the past, future, or other dimension is safe from time travel with computers. With time travel with information no computer file on earth is safe. Some in the government would call that a national security threat but the user who has that information cannot verify it very easily they only know it is a possible result like in the penny experiment.

Still, no one wants there files on their computer reconstructed on someone else's computer so easily. And, it is not against the law because no security was violated. No computer was hacked. No force was used. Nothing was connected too. It's legal to hack this way. Now, if someone gets caught with this information on their hard drive more so if it is NSA or CIA material then yeah, there may be some legal problems and issues and a lot of questions. But understand this is a method of time-travel with computers. These numbers from 0 to 255 can approximate analog signals of light and sound from the future or the past.

In essence producing a machine that is capable of spying on the dinosaurs as they lived millions of years ago or a women in the privacy of her own home all though her property nor her home was never violated. No one was there with a camera. But all information exist in the informational universe so like the video of the dinosaurs her video too exist in the informational universe even though it was never filmed. This technology can be used for good or for evil.

A computer file can be constructed that exist on another computer without ever connecting to that computer. And, no matter where that file is in space or time no file is safe from time travel with computers. No file can hide or run from it. No matter what data someone or the government has on a computer my methods of time travel can reconstruct that file. And, no one nor the government would never know it happened. And no one or the government could stop it. Now what are the chances of me constructing a specific file from another computer? Some would say none. They would say the chances can't be greater than getting hit by a tornado or piece of space junk. To that I say it is possible to do with my methods which I will talk about later in this book.

Now here is the advantage my software has over the penny experiment. The complexity of the result obtained from my software is exponentially greater than the results of the penny experiment. Because the results of my software is exponentially greater than using pennies makes using my method of time travel exponentially worth while verses using pennies. Which means there is great value in using my method of time travel. Had Nazi Germany used a computer and my software to find the technology to build a F-16 during world war two the outcome of the war may have been different. This is why the complexity of the result from my software is so important.

Science has postulated Time Travel with Computers is real

Science for years has postulated that time travel with computers is real and can happen. My books of course will show and prove time travel with computers has happened and everyone in the world can be time travelers using my methods.

Science has showed that it is possible to use simulators to show what may have happened in the past. The people who study dinosaurs have used simulators to simulate dinosaurs to find out their biology. I would think that qualifies as time travel with computers.

Science has talked about many different ways to use computers to time travel. My way that I time travel with computers is not the only way but I believe my methods are the best way to time travel with computers. With my methods no detail about the future or the past or other dimensions is safe. Nothing in space-time can hide from my methods of time travel with computers.

Through the worm hole is a popular TV series that showed time travel with computers is possible. That is just one example. And in the mass media from time to time an article appears about time travel with computers.

Myths/Legends/Truth about Time Travel

Government Experiments with Time Travel

It has been rumored that the USA is conducting classified experiments with time travel for years. But there is no way to ever know. Of course the government won't comment. Many people have come forward under the disclosure project as witnesses against the government but of course that has gone nowhere. If you do not know what the disclosure project is it is a public project to get the government to come clean about UFO's, free energy, and to declassify some of its secret high technology. Which has about as much chance of happening as me winning the next presidential election.

Philadelphia Experiment

The Philadelphia Experiment used a battle ship with high energy generators on it around the deck to wrap space around it and make it invisible. Sailors melted into the deck. Some sailors disappeared only to reappear elsewhere in space-time. And the entire shipped moved from one place to another. It was considered a failed experiment because at the time they only wanted to make the ship invisible. The technology from that experiment was said to later be used in new very secret classified programs.

Remarkable a man by the name John Hutchinson on the Internet was able to reproduce some of the effects in the experiment with the Hutchinson Effect. He has showed wood and metal melting together and floating objects off the ground. His videos have appeared on YouTube. His lab was raided several times and his equipment taken to be studied. But the Hutchinson Effect reproduced some of the effects in the Philadelphia Experiment which tells me that Hutchinson verified the stories about people melting into metal and other strange things that happened on that ship. It is no wonder Hutchinson got his lab raided so many times and his equipment taken from him.

Project Looking Glass

Project looking glass is said to be a project that looks like a gyro-scope and has high energy towers around it. It allows the occupant to look forward or backward in time to see events as they unfold. It is a black budget shadow government project that no one not even the president is supposed to know about. But somehow its existence was leaked to the public.

Photos on the Internet

There has been many good photos pop up on the Internet showing people out of place for their time period. One such photo has a man with an advanced digital camera wearing a screen printed shirt at a time with those things did not exist. Someone once said if time travel is possible where the time travelers now? They are out there but people just have to know where and how to look for them. I think some pictures do not lie and tell a truth that cannot be denied.

Time Travel in the Movies

Time travel in the movies which is considered fiction sometimes depict methods of time travel that have been considered theoretical in real life. Most of the shows have a specific device. Other shows used less real means of time travel which made the show that much more fictional. But, some of the shows even though the method of time travel was ridiculous turned out to be fun and enjoyable. Mainly because the show had such good characters and a plot to the movie that made them even the more enjoyable. Such examples as "The Time Travelers Wife" where the time traveler had a genetic condition that made him time-travel. Bill and Ted's excellent adventure where they traveled in a phone booth which resembled doctor who which also had a time traveling phone booth.

Some of the really good ones was back to the future which became series of movies. Star Trek was famous for its time travel. Terminator which also became a movie series. Then there was Looper. There were many other still pretty good time travel movies. Lately I have watched Project Almanac and then another one I want to see is called Dimensions. In Dimensions some of the theory in the movie resembled my own theories such as what has happened will happen again. In the new Battle Star galactic the same theory of what has happened before will happen again was echoed throughout the movie series.

There is a point where fiction becomes science. Humans going to the moon and mars was considered fiction and there where many movies made about that. But now going to the moon and mars has become science. We are still waiting for men to go to mars. God forbid the apocalypse does not come before men make it to mars. As most people know the earth is going through climate change that is threatening to turn our planet into a desert with no water. We may yet make it to the stars if current projects don't get canceled. But, as the planet warms the oceans water will escape to outer space and other horrible things will happen as time goes along. But for today society still goes on. It is not over till the fat lady sings just yet.

Time Travel with Computers and Information

This part of the book is the reason I wrote this book in the first place. In order for me to help others understand my method of time travel it was necessary for me to talk about all aspects of time travel in depth. To set the scene and the stage where I can present my method of time travel here.

History of Time Travel with Computers and Information

Many people who may have read my previous books know how I got the idea for BNS. I was sitting in class in high school in electrons at vocational college and my instructor was going over scientific notation. I wanted to invent a system to replace scientific notation. Well that led me on a journey to invent a new numerical system. Then I read Einstein's work and applied his work to my own VCNS (Vector Coordinate Numerical System) and BNS (Burris Numerical System) was born to store information in space and time.

Later long after high school I was building a website about things nuclear. I had a fascination with nuclear energy. My website was called "How to build a homemade nuclear reactor". That earned me the name "Reactor1967. On the Internet. Well long story short one day I was trying to do some research on the Internet and what I was trying to I find out had been largely banned and censored information. So, I was not going to very easily include that information in my web-sight. I searched and searched the internet but ever where I searched the information had been removed from the public eye. What I wanted to know was forbidden and censored information. Man was I upset. I thought what right does anyone has to tell me what information I can see or not see. Oh I was hot.

Well here I go again. Just like the time in high school when I wanted to fix the limits of scientific notation I was sitting at my computer saying to myself. Man, "There must be a way around information bans". I remembered my BNS and how I stored information in space and time and I said to myself. Now, if I can store information into space and time how do I search space and time for information?

I was tired of living in a bubble on the Internet. I was tired of other people telling me what I could search for and could not search for. I was tired of people on the internet telling me what I had a right to see and know and what I did not have a right to see and know. Well me being the computer nerd I am I came up with the idea of data-mining a binary counter and later discovered the informational universe then later on honed and refined my theory of time travel with computers to include weak and strong check-sums thinks to a program called Rsync.

Later on down the road after I got better at writing binary counters and search bots to data mine those counters my problems with searching for and finding information that I wanted to know was over. The only thing is I found out was that if something is banned then I run into another problem of not being able to verify the information I have found very easily. It is dang hard to verify something WHEN IT IS CLASSIFIED, BANNED, AND CENSORED!!! But at least I can see the information and make my own decisions. At least I have it in my hands and in front of my face and on my computer where before I did not even have that much.

So, yeah I can search for things but I can't always verify it. More so if it is incredibly complicated. And, somethings I find are so far in the future I don't have any way to verify it at all. The science and the tools to apply that kind of science do not exist yet so I am out of luck there too. Nano-technology is one of those things. Today I am still trying to piece information together. But it is still fun. I am not in a freaking search bubble any more. In fact I get to look at information the CIA, NSA, and the military can only dream about and drool over. Not even the president has access to the information I have seen.

Then there is the problem of finding information with dates on it like 2025, 2050, 3025 way the heck into the future. It did not take me long when I first started this to understand what I was doing was time traveling with computers. My experiments started out on text counters and emails and my A/B system and later moved to more advanced computer files and systems for computer temporal applications.

Later my experiments with time travel with computers went into temporal communication and temporal parallel computing and methods for trying to bring temporal computing into REAL TIME COMPUTER APPLICATIONS. The list of things that can be done with time travel with computers goes on and on and on.

One of my experiments I did one time with my A/B system of temporal communication was I wrote a program where a bunch of balls bounced around on the screen. I had each ball assigned a counter and it was data mining that counter for messages to itself in the future telling the balls when they collided with another ball. At those coordinates the balls would change direction to avoid a collision. If the balls avoided a collision based on this information then CAUSALITY WAS VIOLATED!!! I worked with that program a long time and got those balls avoiding a lot of collisions and flashing and beeping every time one of my balls VIOLATED CAUSALITY!!! It was the one program that I wrote that actually to prove causality can be violated with time travel with computers. Yes indeed causality can be violated with the penny theorem.

And so with time travel with computers causality can be violated because quantum uncertainty does not prevent the present from knowing the future or the past. We can with time travel with computers see our future. We can communicate with our future. We can search for knowledge from the future and bring it here to the past.

We can also search for long lost information from the past and bring it to the future. No one has ever seen a video of a real live dinosaur. With time travel with computers it is possible to find such a video. To find many videos like that to study this creature as it really was in real life.

It is also possible to find ancient scrolls lost in history and war. They can be recovered as special files with special fonts or with pictures.

BNS – Burris Numerical System

Burris Numerical System uses time and space to represent numbers

I will try not to rehash everything I wrote in my first two books but it must be mentioned here that my first foray into time travel with computers was with BNS. BNS started it all for me. It showed me what we really are in space and time. It to me explains some of the universe and gives me a better understanding of why I am here. What my purpose is here on earth. Where I am going in the future. BNS helped me to understand it all.

If anyone has ever had the chance to run my best BNS programs they would see the beauty of space-time as it relates to information. One of my videos on YouTube shows BNS coding data when I hit the decode key BNS decodes the data. I am Reactor1967 on YouTube if anyone wants to find it.

Here is the beauty about that program. It just codes binary 1's and 0's. One can run that program for 1000 years if one has a computer that will run that long. And, when one hits decode then for the next one thousand years all the data that was encoded in BNS will spend the next one thousand years being decoded. DOES ANYONE KNOW HOW MUCH DATA THAT IS? AND THE BEAUTY OF IT IS THAT THE COMMUTER DID NOT STORE A SINGLE BIT OF THAT DATA. The program recovered the data by only keeping the last digit in the number it encoded the data in. It did not keep the rest of the numbers!

So, a number or data that took one thousand years to code and one thousand years to decode was done so with only keeping the last digit in that number. Where was the rest of that number stored during that time? Using Einstein's principles of his relativity theory the rest of the number was mathematically stored in time not space. That is right. Time was used as the hard drive to store information instead of space.

That BNS program is even a bigger hit than calculating pie. Too bad much of current science does not know about it yet or does not care because I am not an academic. Now anyone can run that program 1 hour and it will take 1 hour to decode. How long someone runs it is up to them. But, no matter how long the data stream is it can and will always be recovered without storing it on a computer. No matter how long the program is ran the data stream can always be recovered. Mathematically it is possible to store every piece of information in the universe on BNS on any computer the problem is how much time is there to do it? With BNS time not space is the only constraining factor. But, time is also the greatest force in the universe. It catches up with everyone and everything even the universe itself. So, yes it is possible to use BNS to store data but it is not possible to use BNS to store all the data in the universe. But, that is where my time travel with computers comes into play. With that we don't have to store everything we can search for what we want.

Informational Universe

There is a universe that exist outside of our own. This universe is called the informational universe. In this universe is all the information that is possible to exist in this universe. In the informational universe is our own past, future, and alternate time lines. In this universe there exist every video of every day of one's life from their birth to their death. In this universe exist every email anyone has ever written or will receive. In this universe is every TV show everyone will watch and every movie everyone will watch. In this informational universe is every detail of everybody's life from birth to death.

Also, in this informational universe is every computer file on every place or time known to exist in the universe in the past, present, future, and alternate time-lines. The informational universe can be created on a computer and traveled like a time traveler would really travel the universe. The informational universe can be used as a time machine to see all of space and time with no limits or laws preventing anyone from accessing that information. No one can be tracked by the government in the informational universe. No one's IP in the informational universe can be logged and traced. No one will know for sure what has downloaded from the informational universe unless they get into someone's computer of course who downloaded it.

The informational universe is the ultimate way to time travel with computers. All one has to have is the software and know how to run it. The informational universe will exist forever. It will never go away because space and time is a continuum that cannot ever go away. As long as space-time exist the informational universe will exist. So, the informational universe is also a continuum in its own right.

Cosmos infinite universe infinite worlds

The cosmos is an infinite universe with infinite worlds. Every possible life form that can exist does exist in the cosmos. Every possible earth with every possible time-line exist in the cosmos. Every possible person exist in the cosmos. The word infinite cannot come close to saying what is out there.

Has anyone ever sat on a mountain and wondered at the beauty of our planet? Now, imagine how many worlds out there and how many beautiful landscapes exist with infinite combinations of life.

Now imagine being able to set at a computer and look for computer media files of those landscapes. No it is not possible to be there in person. Like the penny experiment no one may know where in the space-time continuum those landscapes existed but none the less they can be viewed like the results from the penny experiment was viewed for the results one would get for the next day at 1pm when the penny was flipped. This is like going on vacation and taking pictures except we stayed home and made the pictures come to us instead.

My theory of information and space time.

In my theory of information and space time here it is as a list.

1. Space-time is a continuum.
2. There is no such thing as the future or the past.
3. There is an informational universe that exist.
4. A computer can be used to travel this informational universe.
5. This method of time travel can be called
   A. Time travel simulator.
   B. 5th dimensional simulator
1. Computers can be hacked without connecting to them.
2. It is possible to use the informational universe as a method of communication with the future or the past or alternate time-lines.
3. It is possible to find technology with time travel with information.
4. It is possible to study the universe with time travel with information.
5. Time travel with information can be used as a weapon of war or to gain advantage over an opponent.
6. Time travel with information can be used to spy on people.

Ideal to data mine binary counters.

A computer file is a list of numbers from 0 to 255. A binary counter is a counter that turns over all those numbers in a file from 0 to 255. A binary counter is a counter where each digit in that counter can be anything from 0 to 255. Now that counter can be any file length from small to large. Say we want to find a file from next week's news program that is 25 Million bytes in size. So our binary counter would have to be 25 million bytes long. That is 25 million numbers that can be from 0 to 255. Now some would say there is no way that would take way to long.

Really, are you sure about that? As you read this book I will show you why that is not impossible. So, we get a method to run this counter. The method I use for this book is a throttled rolling check-sum counter. Now, when I run a counter I always have 2 check-sums.

1. A weak checksum (more about this later in the book.)
2. A strong checksum (more about this later in the book.)

When the counter starts I have 1 weak check-sum but two strong check-sums

1. One source strong check-sum (This is the check-sum the counter starts with.)
2. One destination strong check-sum (This is the check-sum the counter will finish with)

The weak check-sum stays the same for the counter until the strong destination check-sum is reached. After that all new check-sums are loaded onto the counter. The weak check-sum can stay the same and the source strong check-sum can stay the same but the destination strong check-sum will always change.

The binary counter is the source check-sum that I roll to the destination strong check-sum. The destination can be a known media file or an unknown time travel media file.

When the destination strong check-sum is reached the counter is saved out to a file with the appropriate file extension and the counter is reloaded for another file construction run.

Now where do I get my check-sums? I get them either from known computer media or by mathematically calculating them.

Some-times with this method I only find partial media files which I have to finish re-constructing and some-times I find whole files which do not need to be finished re-constructing. This process will not find a perfect file every time but can get close enough to be of value. Partial files can be reconstructed by moving the destination strong check-sum counter in small increments until the complete file is reconstructed.

When my program runs the output looks like this in the terminal window.

Source check-sum 23.837432938 Weak check-sum 723847327434389
Strong check-sum 30.987438987 Weak check-sum 723847327434389
Source check-sum 24.837432938 Weak check-sum 723847327434389
Strong check-sum 30.987438987 Weak check-sum 723847327434389
Source check-sum 25.837432938 Weak check-sum 723847327434389
Strong check-sum 30.987438987 Weak check-sum 723847327434389
Source check-sum 26.837432938 Weak check-sum 723847327434389
Strong check-sum 30.987438987 Weak check-sum 723847327434389
Source check-sum 27.837432938 Weak check-sum 723847327434389
Strong check-sum 30.987438987 Weak check-sum 723847327434389
Source check-sum 28.987438987 Weak check-sum 723847327434389
Strong check-sum 30.987438987 Weak check-sum 723847327434389
Source check-sum 29.987438987 Weak check-sum 723847327434389
Strong check-sum 30.987438987 Weak check-sum 723847327434389
Source check-sum 30.987438987 Weak check-sum 723847327434389
File Reconstructed!!!!!!!!

Here is a picture of my program in action

Target strong check-sum

File constructed

Source strong check-sum

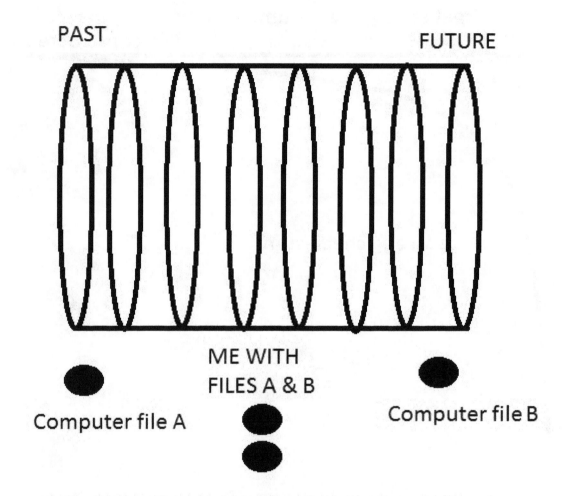

SPACE-TIME

PAST

FUTURE

ME WITH
FILES A & B

Computer file A

Computer file B

ACCORDING TO EINSTEIN ALL OF SPACE-TIME
EXIST HERE AND NOW. THE PAST EXIST NOW AND
THE FUTURE EXIST NOW. OUR PERCEPTION OF
TIME CAN ONLY SEE THE PRESENT BUT THERE IS
NO LAW OF PHYSICS THAT PREVENTS US FROM
KNOWING THE PAST OR THE FUTURE NOW!!!

Now as this counter offloads files I have other programs watching the offloaded files. The other programs are testing the offloaded files for a video file format. I have a program extracting video frames from the found video files as it hits videos checking the quality of the video frames. You name it.

I have a system on the counter that allows the counter to run very fast and slow down when the destination strong check-sum is coming into range.

This is called data mining a binary counter. This is called searching the informational universe.

Data mining counters for access to informational universe

There are many ways to data mine a binary counter to gain access to the informational universe. There is no one best method for that. There are many ways to run a binary counter and again there are many ways to data mine it.

I am going to in this book talk about a lot of things but I am going to talk about one method which I kept simple and elegant that will help the reader understand how to data mine binary counter to gain access to the informational universe. The method I choose for this book is the throttled rolling check-sum counter. The counter with one weak check-sum and a starting strong check-sum called the source and the finishing strong check-sum called the destination. This counter method is simple and best for the public and is not overly complicated.

Now, when data mining a binary counter a person can get many copies of files where each file is a little different than the last file. The quality of the file can get better or worse as the counter rolls. It is possible to find two copies of the same file at different weak check-sums with one copy being better than the other.

It is easy to fill up a hard drive up with files when data mining a binary counter so one needs tools and programs to help sort through the massive mess of files. One can get a lot of junk files too or can find a diamond in the hay stack. Anything is possible with data mining a binary counter. It is a computer intensive job and will require a lot of work and time if one is serious about this. But, anything worth having is worth working for. What I do requires a particular mind set. So far I have never met anyone that has a passion for this like I do. It takes a lot of skill, work, and a desire.

When I started doing this I mainly filled up my hard drive with files. I spent hours searching and looking through files. As time went along I got better at it and wrote better code. I found automating this process is the best way to be successful.

Data mining counters instead of discovery and invention

It is possible to data mine a counter for discovery and invention. Once programs have been written to run the counter and run the search bots then one needs to sit down and do a very serious mathematical study to determine where at on the binary country a search will be done. This needs to be done first before the programs can be run.

I use to use known computer media files to find the range of strong destination check-sums for each specific weak check-sum. Then I would take the root mean square of known strong destination check-sums for the known media and the high standard deviation and the low standard deviation and I could calculate a search area where unknown computer media files would be in for specific weak and strong destination check-sums.

After that it was just a matter of getting the binary counter to roll to all those weak and strong destination check-sums and use my search bots to look for unknown time travel computer media. Sometimes I could find a whole file and sometimes I would find a partial file that I would have to go back and reconstruct.

It is not necessary to do years and years of research and spend millions or billions of dollars for scientific research when one can just program a binary counter and program search bots to search the informational universe for the technology that is being looked for. It is far cheaper to search for the technology in the informational universe and test the technology in the real world than it is to invent it. And as the technology of searching a binary counter gets better and better so would the benefits from using that technology.

Data mining counters for time hacking

My method of time travel can also be thought of as time hacking. In essence I am using a binary counter like a hacker would use to crack a web page or some ones password. But, now using the binary counter to find computer media of the future, past, or alternate time lines. I in all rights could be called a time-hacker. This is using hacking to hack space-time. To hack the continuum. And yes, in a sense hacking gods computer.

Also, my software can be considered a time-travel simulator, a fifth dimension simulator, a time machine, time travel with a computer. You see using binary counters to construct unknown files by constructing their weak and strong check-sums it is possible to recreate files that exist on other computers but without ever connecting to that other computer. That means emails, personal files, and files with information that is supposed to be kept secret. This is a perfect legal way to hack computers because no laws are being broken.

I am a hacker that hacks the continuum to look for time travel computer media files or just to look for files that are on other peoples computers in the past, future, or alternate time-lines. And, many do not know this but this can be a form of temporal communication with the past, future, or alternate time-lines with the right setup. More about that up ahead in this book. This is hacking at its finest and highest degree. The ultimate way to hack. To hack god's computer and steal his files is the ultimate achievement for a hacker. When you can hack god himself then you have become the most dangerous hacker that mankind or the continuum has ever known.

Four methods of time travel with computers and information

1. A/B algorithm temporal communication system protocol.
2. Finding time travel computer media of the past, present, future, or alternate time-lines/dimensions.
3. Temporal parallel computing.
4. Approximating analog signals of the past, present, future, or alternate timelines/other dimensions.

A/B algorithm temporal communication protocol

My algorithm for communications with the past future, or alternate time-lines, even with others in the present:

If A in the past, and B in the future both know the weak and strong check-sum range

C high end of the range

D low end of the range

That their messages to each other through space and time will be in. Then B in the future can construct a message to A in the past between the known check-sum range C & D.

After B constructs this message B then will save a copy of course then delete it.

Now, A in the past using a binary counter to constructs messages between the check-sum ranges C and D can find the message that B in the future sent to A in the past.

Now, A in the past can reply to this message and save a copy and delete it. Then B in the future using a binary counter to construct the messages between check-sum range C and D can find the message A in the past sent to B in the future.

Both A in the past and B in the future using this system of communication can talk to each other. This system of communication does not depend on distance, it does not depend on time. Two people in parallel universes could talk to each other using this system.

Two people across the galaxy from each other. Can use it. Even people trillions of years apart in time apart can use it. You see, it is also possible to use this system to find others to talk to who use it too. This type of communication can be very simple or extremely advanced.

Temporal Email System

The A/B algorithm can be used as a temporal email system as I explained. Now, this system can use encryption codes and algorithms to verify the sender and receiver of the message. It is possible to use quantum particle entanglement as a verification system for the messages. I don't work in a lab advanced enough to test this out so I will just throw that out there for the diehard scientist who have the resources to research this. With this verification system the message would contain the results of the particle entanglement and the scientist would confirm the particle entanglement to confirm the message is real.

Now, my DIY method is to use events on my own time-line between myself in the past and myself in the future to verify the message. Of course myself and I we used our own brand of encryption to encrypt our messages to each other but myself in the future would tell me of events in my future.

As the events happened then I could verify the message I found to myself was indeed true in the past. Now, me in the past communicating with myself in the future could only include events that myself in the future would of course know of thus myself in the future verified the message from myself in the past was true based on known past events that I spoke about in my message.

Plus, I also remembered writing the message in the past so that helped me too. I would find messages that I remembered sending to myself in the future. Now if I was communicating with someone else then of course all I could do was recite events in my time-line.

And, using my BNS and my strong and weak check-sums I could embed file attachments in the messages and myself in the future or the past could decode those attachments. I could see myself as I got older. Know of things that might happen to me in the future. My other self would see himself younger and see things in the past he had long forgotten about.
This is a perfectly good way to communicate with other people in other space-times. I call this temporal Email. My A/B algorithm is the crutch of all my temporal communication systems.

Real Time Temporal Communication

If the computer can find the messages fast enough this could be used for Real-Time communication. You see, the messages do not just have to be text. They can also be video and audio. The A/B algorithm can search for video and play it then one says what they have to say and the computer would record it then look for a response to what was just said.

With a fast enough computer and the right file formats and the right protocols used this could be a real-time live communication with another person in the past, future, or alternate time-lines. Even in the present if no other form of communication existed. If a computer can search fast enough for the videos between the C and D check-sum range of my algorithm and verify them fast enough then the sender and receiver could speak and meet at the appropriate times with each other in their own time-lines.

It is a very weird way to communicate but it can be done. Now, if it was possible to crunch people into information and embed them into a message and the receiver could on the other side reconstruct that individual from that information then sending people to the future, past, or alternate time-lines would be possible. But In theory you would only be sending a copy of a person and in theory receiving a copy of a person. No mass nor energy could make the trip only information could make the trip. There was a movie where this was done to send people across the universe but after the information was sent the copy of the person left behind was destroyed. Which became a problem for the people in the movie after they found out. In the movie it was called balancing the equation.

Temporal Parallel Computing

I spoke about communication in real time with the past or the future or alternate time-lines. But also there is another type of communication. A parallel computer using my methods of time travel as it is processing its information can also use my A/B algorithm to see if its future self has found a result and if it has then retrieve that result from the future and resets its calculations it is running to use that result thus using temporal communication to jump ahead and finish its calculations quicker and faster.

This is called parallel temporal computing. Using the Burris A/B algorithm it is possible to take a slow computer and make it faster than the world's fastest super computer.

The computer would be programed to run the binary counters and the search bots but the counter and the search bots would be programmed to look for and run the parallel temporal problem. It would not be too much different than parallel computers today but the computer would search the counter for messages it sent or received from itself in the future, past, or other dimensions concerning the parallel problem. It would have a protocol about how to handle these messages and verify them then use the result to jump ahead in its calculations.

Finding Time Travel Computer Media

In the last few years I have experimented with dozens of types of counters for searching for time travel computer media. Instead of trying to explain each and every counter for the purpose of this book and to save my readers countless hours of aggravation I am going to follow the KISS RULE. Keep it simple stupid. I will be able to teach my readers how to time travel and save many problems down the road.

There is an old program called Rsync. This program backed up data over a weak internet connection using weak and strong check-sums to re-construct a computer file. Now, the crutch of my time travel with computers is being able to (re-construct a computer file). The difference between Rsync and I is Rsync only wants to re-construct known files in the present. I want to construct files from the past, present, future, and other time lines. Also Rsync used a list of weak and strong check-sums where I use just one weak and one strong destination check-sum.

So, early on I realized I could use Rsync's methodologically with my own methodologically. So, that is what I did. I wrote a counter where I could give the counter a weak check-sum and a strong check-sum and it would construct the file. But, what I did after that was brand new and is why I try to mathematically calculate check-sums of files that exist in the past, present, future, and alternate time-lines. My counters do not care when or why the files existed all my counters do is take the check-sums I give it and construct the files. My penny rules of time travel are persevered. My penny law of time travel with information is preserved.

So, starting out I wrote a program that could take a known file in the present and write a configuration file with the strong and weak check-sums and the file size. It would write this information to a text file. My counter program would load the text file and use the check-sums to reconstruct the media file.

Now, I wrote a third program that just writes configuration files that may have check-sums of time travel media files. This program passes these configuration files to my file reconstruction program which constructs these files.
Now, my data mining robots take over and go through these files to verify that they are indeed real files that belong somewhere else in space-time or even exist in the present on another computer somewhere.

With these programs anyone anywhere with a computer can time travel.

Approximating Analog Signals of other Space-Times

In the world of open source there is the GNU open source radio project. The project uses software to process analog radio signals then the minimum amount of hardware needed to receive and broadcast those signals. This software uses digital to analog converters and analog to digital converts. The software does the main bulk of the work. This is called GNU RADIO.

This system of using software to approximate analog signals is not new and has been around for a long time. The software that I talk about in this book to search the continuum for time travel media is also capable of approximating analog signals of light and audio from other times and places. So, when a valid time travel computer media video file is found it could easily be a video of the Jurassic or any other part of earth's history. It is also possible the video could be of another time and place on another planet in the universe. Even of another time and place that existed before or after this present universe. Somewhere in the history of space-time itself. Because the software was designed to access the informational universe of space-time itself is what makes this possible. So, this process is called "Time-Travel Approximating Analog Signals".

Components of Time Travel with Information

The methods I use to time travel with information have many components. I will do a brief outline then try to explain some of them.

1. Tools (These are programs I use to setup a time travel project and extract information from it.
2. Check-sum hacking. Without this there would be no time travel with information at all.
3. Data-Mining. Now we have to data mine the files we check-summed hacked.
4. Verification. This goes for verifying communications as well as for time travel media files.

5. File attachments. Some messages from the future or past have file attachments with them.

1. Tools:

These are some of my programs like BNS which can store a lot of information as a couple of numbers. This is useful for file attachments in my A/B algorithm where I can look for messages to myself from the future that have very large files. There are programs that I use to set up projects. One of my programs will take a list of files and compute the root mean square and standard deviation of the check-sums. So, if I want to find more files like those I look at check-sums that fall within the standard deviation. Other programs will give me a strong check-sum and weak check-sum of a specific file. I have programs for ripping the file format from two or more files that I use in my verify programs. On tools I would also have check-sum bots to generate check-sums for me. I would have encryption bots to verify encryption or crack encryption that I may find in a time travel media file. Oh yes I have not talked about it very much but sometimes I find files that have encryption and I have to verify that it is encrypted then go about trying to break that encryption to get to the secrets inside the file.

2. Check-sum hacking:

This is the science of taking a weak check-sum and a strong check-sum and running check-sum counters to reconstruct the computer file. This is the back bone of time travel with information. Now, everyone remember that penny experiment. Here I run the counter to try to construct unknown computer files that can exist in the future or the past. No law in physics prevents the future or past from being known but it is damn hard to physically time travel. Here I don't worry about it we just try to find the time travel computer media by constructing files from unknown check-sums. And the same check-sum hacking program can be used to back up a computer to a list of check-sums called fire codes. So that in the event the hard drive is lost a person can use the check-sums and reconstruct their files on their new computer.
Now with data mining I need algorithms for running the counters. Algorithms for speeding the counters up and slowing them down. I need algorithms for computing the weak and strong check-sums and so on.

3. Data Mining:

Now, once I start reconstructing files from unknown check-sums the hard drive will start filling up. There will be thousands and thousands of files. When I first started doing this I was very overwhelmed. I could only look at a very small fraction of the files so I had to write robots to data mine the files and pick out the best ones and save them for later. Now on data mining I check for misspelled words, syntax, file attachments, file formats, verification codes. I also have a search engine I can setup to search the reconstructed files for specific content. Data mining won't be optional if someone tries to recreate my work. Also I forgot to mention it is very useful to have an artificial intelligent data mining robot laying around for this job. An AI that can be trained to perform specific task that is best performed by a neural net.

4. Verification:

The found time travel media and the found time travel messages now need to be verified. This gets a little harder to do. On the A/B algorithm the sender and receiver can set up a code a verification method but the other media files have to be physically looked at and now someone has to play detective. It is not always easy and nor is it always possible to verify the files. Here the person playing detective would set up a folder system and work on the media files like a detective would work on a case.

5. File attachments:

This is my favorite part of my A/B temporal message system. Found messages can contain videos, computer files, you name it from the future. For me this is like opening up a present at Christmas time except I get to do it all the time. This part never ever gets old for me.

Setting up Time Travel Projects

Here I will try to discuss the technical details as much as possible about how I setup a time travel computer programs.

Beginning of a project:

What I do at the beginning of a project is I try to collect known computer media first similar to the media I will be looking for. The reason I do this is I can use the known computer media to find the range of check-sums I want to search. One of my first projects was trying to find newspaper headlines. So for months I got the daily newspaper and I cut out the front page and I scanned the front page to a picture. I did this until I had more pictures of newspaper headlines than I knew what to do with.

Now for finding messages from the future, past, or alternate timelines. If someone was using my A/B algorithm the first step would be to set down and write a message to themselves every day in the past until they had a collection of messages they could use.

Using tools:

After collecting the pictures and or writing myself messages I would use my tools to find my root mean square and standard deviation of the check-sum range I will be searching in. This included the weak and strong check-sums.

Setting up counters:

Now once I know my search range I can program my counters to run within a check-sum range. That would be the weak and strong check-sum range. My programs would construct the possible strong check-sums for each specific weak check-sum within that range.

Setting up data mining search bots:

Here I would use my tools to rip file formats and setup other kinds of checks like video frame checks. On the file formats my program would just compare the counter file to the file format file to see if the counter file had a file format. My program just compares files for that. If using text files I would get my spell and syntax bots ready to look at files and do stuff with them mainly to see how many correct words and a percentage of the correct syntax. If I found text with mostly correct words and syntax my bots would save it for me to look at it later. This is no small thing here. Often I have to re-write code and recompile for the type of search I was doing.

Running the project Programs:

After everything is setup and configured I start my counter and run my bots at the same time then I monitor my output directories.

Creating an informational search engine:

This whole process I just explained can be used to setup a time-travel search engine. After all the files are checked the ones that passed would be put into a directory and the final program could search those files like a search engine. Or as the files are created they could be searched then deleted if they don't match the profile. Some-times it is just beneficial to set down and open up these files before they are deleted to see what is being thrown away. But, when running a massive operation of course that is not always possible.

Programming bots and counters to act together:

The bots and counters have to know when to take a break and when to work. So I programed them to keep up with the number of files in the directory. I have over ran my computer space before.

Verify the results and Use the information:

This is not as simple as it may seem. It can be hard to verify everything and how one will use what they find often has to be handled delicately.

I have ran this whole process before for months at a time. Usually I had to replace hard drives every so often. One time I woke up with fire shooting out the back of my PC power supply as my PC power supply went out. I have never seen that happen before but it did. This whole process usually works better if the user knows how's to code and run rolling check-sum counters and can fix her or his own computer equipment.

How to create and run a throttled rolling check-sum counter

Now, this may very well be the most important part of this book a lot of my readers have been waiting for. An algorithm to run a rolling check-sum counter. If you read this book waiting for this information then I appreciate your patience. If someone is trying to recreate my work then this part is very important for them.

How a rolling check-sum counter works. A rolling check-sum counter has these functions to do.

1. Add
2. Subtract
3. Switch and subtract
4. Carry
5. Roll

Rules for running the rolling check-sum counter.

1. Whatever is added must be subtracted
2. Whenever nothing can be added or subtracted then add and subtract is switched places. Then subtract 1 from subtract. Then if one can carry a one in the carry section then a carry will be performed. If the carry can't be performed then a roll is performed to the counter then a carry will be performed at the end of the roll. A roll is where all the bytes are shifted over and the end of the counter becomes the front of the counter. The counter always stays the same weak check-sum. But the strong source check-sum will change until it equals the destination strong check-sum.

Now where my counters differ is I use base math. I don't just add and subtract 1. I add and subtract very large numbers to and from my counters to quickly roll it to a specific strong check-sum. If I add three bytes I subtract three bytes. If I had 100 bytes to the counter I subtract 100 bytes from the counter. My Roll in bytes is always the same amount of bytes I am adding and subtracting. But my switch still only subtracts 1 and my carry only adds 1. After a roll always finish the carry or the counter will be out of range on its weak check-sum.

I break my binary counter down into sections.

SECTIONS OF COUNTER:
Rest of Counter, Carry, Add, Subtract.
<<<<<<<<<< Roll counter in this direction <<<<<<<<<<<<<<<<

SECTIONS OF COUNTER:
Subtract, Add, Carry, Rest of Counter
>>>>>>>>>>Roll counter in this direction >>>>>>>>>>>>>>>

The counter operations up above are performed in the direction of the arrows.

When rolling the counter the sections of the counter do not move. The sections are where mathematical operations are performed. When the counter rolls the roll is performed on every single byte in the counter. No section of the counter remains un-rolled.

So again I will repeat myself. What is added must be subtracted. When an add or subtract cannot be performed add and subtract is switched and 1 is subtracted but instead of adding 1 a carry of one is performed to the counter. If a carry cannot be performed because the byte is maxed out then the counter is rolled. After the roll then the carry is performed. When I roll the counter I roll it the length of the bytes I was previously adding or subtracting. If I was adding and subtracting 3 bytes then I roll the counter 3 bytes. When I start building a strong check-sum I start my counter off at a small speed then increase the speed of the counter. By speed I mean I increase how much I am adding or subtracting from the counter. I start by adding and subtracting 1. Then I multiply that by a specific amount till I pass up my destination check-sum. I restore the counter to its previous state then I reduce how much I am adding and subtracting by a percentage until I am no longer passing up the strong check-sum. Each time I pass up the strong check-sum I restore the counter and reduce my speed again until the strong destination check-sum is reached.

When creating my counter before I use it I put the entire weak check-sum at the beginning of the counter file and the rest of the counter just contains zero's. So, as the strong check-sum is built the weak check-sum gets distributed from the beginning of the counter to the end of the counter until the strong destination check-sum is created/reached for that specific weak check-sum.

Example weak check-sum 510 Starting out with:

255, 255, 0 but as the counter runs it will look like this 250, 250, 10

Now this is getting a little advanced for this book but let's say my counter passes its strong check-sum. I can reverse the process and run my rolling check-sum counter backwards. Or I can back up the counter every-time before a change is made to it and restore it if I pass up my strong check-sum. But then I would need to reduce the speed of the counter. When the strong destination check-sum is passed up reduce the speed of the counter.
So, as my rolling check-sum counter runs it passes up the strong check-sum and I reduce the speed of the counter. The counter is restored to its previous state. The counter goes through a period of where it is building up speed then it goes through a period of where the speed is decreased until the file is constructed. After the counter has obtained its fastest speed as it passes up the strong check-sum the counter is restored to its original condition then the speed of the counter is reduced until the strong source check-sum of the counter matches the strong destination check-sum the counter had intended to build. The speed is only reduced when the counter passes up its strong check-sum instead of hitting it. When the strong check-sum is hit the counter is done reconstructing that file. The counter file is then saved out with its appropriate file extension to be looked at by the bots or a human.

How to compute weak and strong check-sums

Here is how to compute a weak check-sum. $12345 = 1 + 2 + 3 + 4 + 5 = 15$

How to compute a strong check-sum. Here is how I use weights.

$(1 * .3) + (2 * .1) + (3 * .7) + (4 * .9) + (5 * .8) =$ strong check-sum.
Each byte in the counter is assigned one or more weights. The more weights per byte the stronger the check-sum. If one has two or more weights in the strong check-sum then it would look like this.

$(1 * .3) + (1 * .2)$ First byte $+ (2 * .1) + (2 * .4)$ Second Byte .... = Strong check-sum. Again the more weights per byte the stronger the check-sum.

Now the weights can be anything. I use a random number generator to get my weights but I also use a seed to make sure the same weights are generated every time for each byte.

And last I do not cut my check-sums off to a specific length. Whatever their length is: Is what I use. Remember I have my BNS that I can use to code/store my check-sums and to decode/use my check-sums. The length of my check-sums is not an issue for me. It also helps me be deadly accurate for getting really good time travel media files.

Now when all my programs are running I pick a range of weak check-sums to search in. Then I pick a strong check-sum range for each weak check-sum range.

My bot programs generate random strong check-sums for a specific weak check-sum or run a strong check-sum counter and my program constructs files with those strong and weak check-sums. I can pre-program my bots for specific parameters for my weak and strong check-sum search.

My bots generates configure files. Another program runs my reconstruct program with those configure files. Then my robots check-the directories and do their things with the constructed files.

Now for the final part. When I get a partial file I can manually and gently use my reconstruct program to reconstruct the rest of the file. In fact a lot of files I find I have I had to rebuild for one reason or another. I call the partial files counter fragments. A bot should be programed to look for counter fragments too.

Taking a partial file and rebuilding it is a slow process. I usually have my reconstruct program slowly run in one direction building files while my AI checks those files then my AI shuts the process down when the file is reconstructed. All I do is reset my check-sum generator to run slower in one direction in increments and use my AI without the other bots until the file is reconstructed. I also on occasion do run my other bots but over time I have developed my AI to do the job without my other bots.

Advanced Time Travel Simulator

Simulating quantum entanglement with computers.

Time Travel with computers is the embodiment of the subject of entanglement in Physics which is hotly debated. Some people ask if entanglement violates relativity. The answer science gives is no because Entanglement is only transferring Information and has no mass. Which is why my method of time travel works and is time travel. But now the question remains. Does entanglement violate causality? Well the answer to that question is Yes and No. And here is why. For example myself in the future writes a message to myself in the past then deletes it. Myself in the past decodes this message from the future and reads the message. Now what happens? It is like a circle within a circle. One small change in the past changes something else which changes something else. So, for the sake of the argument now my future is basically erased after I read that message from the future. After I read that message that future now no longer exist at least not all of it. So now entanglement has not violated causality at least not completely. Entanglement is like a math equation. When you change one side off the equation you also change the other side of the equation. You cannot change one without the other.

Now after reading the message from the future I make new choices which may mean that in my new future (because my old future was erased) I may have never written that message to myself in my past because now my circumstances have changed. Or, I still might write that message and preserve my time-line and what happened. If I do that then I would be self-fulfilling my destiny. Entanglement in Quantum mechanics is the same way. Basically time travel with computers is actually quantum entanglement in practice with computers and information. Each message from the future is a possible quantum entanglement.

Quantum codes:

So what are quantum codes? Now this is the tricky part. A quantum code is part of the time-line written in a message that was decoded off the binary counter that did not experience entanglement. Yes, it is a part of the time-line that stays preserved after a person reads a message from the future or the past. And now the tricky part. For that code to be good the receiver of that code needs to self-fulfill the future and change as little as possible the events in time after reading the message. Then, while doing so verifies the part of the time-line that did not change thus verifying the quantum code itself thus verifying the message. When the message has been verified as real and the time-line happens the way the message said it would then causality has been violated. This is the yes part of whether or not entanglement can violate causality. Entanglement can only violate causality when there is no entanglement. When there is entanglement the future gets erased thus correcting causality to prevent causality violation.

Entanglement is nature's way of preventing time-travel. But if the time-traveler changes as little as possible the time-line then causality can be violated. But, that can only happen if the time-traveler does not change the time-line or changes as little as possible the time-line. Because once the time-line has changed the future has been erased. Or at least a part of that future has been erased. This is why in quantum mechanics you cannot look at a particle without disturbing it thus changing the way it behaves.

Now, what happens when the future gets erased? Well it is still there but now the future exist in another dimension than the time-traveler. Yes, whenever entanglement happens a new dimension is created where now the new future can exist and the old future is in another dimension separated and safe from causality violation. New dimensions in space-time are created to protect causality. It is another way nature tries to prevent time-travel. When causality is violated then the past and the future still exist in the same dimension because the time traveler preserved the time-line. Only the time-traveler knows what happened. Now after the message has been verified and all the events in time stayed the same then after that the time-traveler can go tell everyone but only after the fact. If he no longer cares what will happen in the future after the message has been verified then he can change whatever he wants.

Now, my method of time-travel is also a popular way to time travel because the main reason people want to time travel is because they want the time-line erased. They want the time-line to change. So, yeah one could use this to change their future but that future will still exist in another dimension but at least the time traveler in the old dimension would benefit from it. The time-traveler in the dimension that was not changed would experience no benefit from this. I would caution against it because and this is serious very serious. One change in the time-line ripples like a small wave which then turns into a giant title wave destroying everything in its path. The future that replaces the old future in the new dimension could be far worse than the first future in the old dimension. So why change the future in the first place?

So far I am the only one I know that time-travels this way. I invented this technology so I could time travel. And my experience with this technology has led me to respect it and use great caution when using my technology for my personal use.

Quantum encryption:

Quantum encryption is simply using encryption with a quantum code. The reason is because we don't want to change the future but preserve it. So, A in the past and B in the future use encryption on their messages to each other so that no one else can receive the message and so that they can verify they are the sender and receiver of their messages to each other.

Real time travel and communication in real time with computers.

Now what happens if A in the past and B in the future want to talk to themselves with each other in real time over video. Some would say this is not possible but as the father of this technology I would say oh yes it is. Oh hell yeah it is possible. But remember A in the past has to not change the time-line or B in the future will never talk to A in the past. Well at least not in the same dimension because entanglement will correct causality if the time-traveler changes anything.

How real time time-travel can happen is by having the counters run on a computer that is fast enough to decode and verify the data stream. Both A in the past and B in the future would need this powerful computer to make this happen.

Temporal parallel computing:

If we have a fast enough pc that can find the messages and verify them quickly we can also employee temporal parallel computing. This is the A/B algorithm but instead of people talking to other people in space-time our computer is talking to itself not only in this dimension but all the other dimensions as well working on a single problem.

Now, if the time traveler's pc is fast enough she or he can write a program to employee temporal parallel computing for the purpose of not only solving all those pesky problems that take tons of computing power but also to use live temporal communication with the future and to even have a blazing fast time-machine for finding computer media of the past or the future and from other dimensions. With this type of machine all information in the universe would be available to the time traveler at the asking. Now, I have not talked about it yet but our rolling check-sum counter can be busted down into smaller counters and ran in parallel to construct a computer media file. How this is done is that each section of the counter would have to fit together so that all the check-sums add up to equal both the weak and strong check-sum.

So, the answer to temporal parallel computing is to write a parallel program to run binary counters then use that program on a parallel computer then use that parallel computer for temporal parallel processing then use the temporal parallel processing as a blazing fast time-machine as well as running it for all those pesky problems that require tons of computing power. Having a computer utilize unlimited dimensions in space-time for parallel processing is the best way to have the fastest computer in the universe as well as a very coveted time-machine.

Temporal computer hacking

This topic I dread talking about because so many people today are fed up with hackers and hacking. But, my methods make it possible to construct computer files that exist on other computers without ever connecting to those computers.

Those violated by this sort of hacking would never know they were hacked until the hacker released the information or used the information in some way. No computer file in the universe is safe from this type of hacking. Not even encrypted data is safe because the hacker can reconstruct it UN-encrypted. This means the hacker can get up every morning and get his NSA/CIA briefing that is only reserved for presidents and the people in the know.

This type of hack is pretty powerful. But it involves the hacker being able to calculate where on the binary counter the data he wants exist. Then using the reconstruct programs to reconstruct that data. He can also use my A/B algorithm to talk to other hackers in other dimensions and in the future and in the past to figure out what he needs to know to get that data. A time-traveler hacker is the world's worst nightmare.

There would be no information the hacker could not get. Including the passwords and security information to crack computers on the Internet in the present. From his time travel with computers the hacker could have the whole Internet as his on personal playground. And he would be able to warn himself in the past so he does not get arrested. This type of hacker would definitely be very feared and hard to catch.

Safety with time travel with information.

Of course over dependence on the information one finds can be a problem. This is a system for exploring space-time but no one should let themselves become dependent upon it. Nature does not make time travel easy even if it is possible. Man has survived this long without time travel and man can continue to survive without again if needed. Taken information and relying on it can cause UN-desired consequences in the time-line that a time traveler did not count on.

Let's say a time traveler wanted to help his mother avoid a traffic accident only to wind up having his entire family in the car and the accident happened anyway later on. So now the time traveler involved his whole family instead of just his mother. When the time-line changes unexpected events can result from that change. Every event in space-time effects other events. On change can change everything.

So, information obtained with my methods must be taken with a grain of salt. There is nothing wrong with trying to change the future but acting on information from time travel can create a paradox where the future that was created was the future trying to be changed. So, that being said life should be lived as it normally would from day to day. Messing with time travel is dangerous. Now that being said again even if someone never hack another computer if they are found with sensitive files like the USA governments classified files then they can still be prosecuted and go to jail for having those files. And that goes for other files as well. Oh let's say someone finds a porn file and they put it on-line and the people in that file see themselves but the whole world now has a copy of that. Those people in that file may feel some kind of way about that and come after the person who posted the file in court. Yep, it can happen. I can't post news media files because of copyright laws even if they are in the future because technically it is still the news stations property. So one has to be careful what files get constructed and kept on a computer with my methods of time travel with information and computers. This can get someone in trouble.

Constructing technology with my methods of time travel.

Anything one builds because they found it will have its own inherent dangers. Everyone is responsible as the builder for their own safety and the safety of those around them. If they build something with my methods of time travel I as the writer I cannot take responsibility for what happens.

Giving away or telling others information learned with time travel with information.

That can have UN-desired consequences for. As I found out when I got on the Internet and talked about it myself. I have been dogged all over the Internet and hacked and even threatened with my life and harassed. So, if anyone tries my methods please realize giving away or talking to others about it can also have its UN-desired consequences. People do not like other people having that kind of power. That kind of knowledge. So, use it with caution. Talk about it with even more caution.

If anyone engages in time travel with information I have learned the hard way to keep everything encrypted and backed up and put away. So, that is my advice for anyone if they try my methods of time travel with computers. Don't act on the information learned from my methods. Don't talk about it. And encrypt and put away those time travel media files. Don't let others see them. That is my advice.

Paradoxes

Now, this would not be a proper time travel book if I did not talk about paradoxes. All the popular TV shows and movies about time travel discuss them. A paradox is where point A in the past observes an event point C in the future and causes the event point B that leads to the event point C in the future. Now if point A had not observed the future it is likely point C may have never happened. Point C only happened because point A time traveled and created that mess in the first place. This is the safety part I talked about previously.

Now, let's look at the reverse of the situation. Point C in the future goes back in time to change point A in the past to prevent point C in the future. But point A creates point B which leads to point C happening anyway. Had not point C time traveled and created the mess in the first place then point C would not have happened either.

So, time travel even with computers and information has its consequences. Any time-travel at all has its own risk. There are just too many variables that a time traveler cannot see nor track.

Conclusion

Time travel can be very informative and entertaining. It is not for the casual user. When using my programs to create files beware there is no filter on this thing. Anything someone can see or hear with my methods can cause emotional or mental distress. Also, some people are not cut out for calculating the weak and strong check-sums a real file may be in. Those people will not find time travel success with my methods of time travel if they cannot calculate the strong check-sum of a real file before creating it. For those people it will be like looking for a needle in a hay stack. They may not find success with time travel with information. Not all people will. I tried to explain all this to a hacker one time I was helping use my methods and that hacker never could get it right even though he himself was a programmer. And at the time I did not know it but this hacker was hacking me to get my computer code. Beware of hackers. They are wolfs in sheep's clothing.

The main secret to making this work is calculating that weak and strong check-sums of computer files that does not exist in the present. I look at known media files to help me. I use statistics and mathematics. I calculate where I am going to search and I construct files within that area of the weak and strong check-sums of my calculations. Sometimes or a lot of times I get a partial file. Now, I have to decide is the strong check-sum weaker or higher. Some-times I need a higher or lower weak check-sum then a higher or lower strong check-sum as well. Here is where the real skill comes in.

I call partial files counter scraps. So, one needs to have data mining setup to save those counter scraps and later they can try to pin point where the correct weak and strong check-sums may be. I use trial and error a lot of times. I try both higher and lower and look at the quality of the file. If it improves in one direction then that direction is the direction I need to go in to find the rest of the file.

One can also find files that look identical but have small differences with each other. Those are alternate reality files. Someone using this would have to decide what reality they like the best. It is possible to get a lot of these files.

This can be a long very boring tedious process but when good files are found from the past, future, or alternate time-lines it is worth it. Even files that exist in the present somewhere then the reward pays for the hard work done.

Think you for reading "How to Time Travel with Computers" and good luck out there to all my fellow time travelers and people who just wanted to read my work. If anyone could tell I am a person who likes to experiment and invent across many subjects. This book was a compilation of my work that I do in private at home. For a long time I thought the public should be made aware of this material. I have put a lot of my personal time and effort into this work and into bringing this work to the public. I want to thank my readers for participating in letting me share this with them.

Computer code for this book:

http://sourceforge.net/projects/firecodes/

http://sourceforge.net/projects/timetravelproject/